Legal Aspects for
Purchasing and Supply

leisure & culture DUNDEE

Working in Partnership
with Dundee City Council

Return to ....REFERENCE AND INFORMATION........................ Library

Please return/renew this item by the last date shown. Items may also be renewed by phone or internet unless requested by another reader.

www.leisureandculturedundee.com/library

Legal Aspects for Purchasing and Supply Chain Management

Ian Longdin LL.M., B.A. (Hons); PGCE

Liverpool AcademicPress

© I. Longdin 2005

First published in Great Britain by Liverpool Academic Press.

A CIP catalogue for this book is available from the British Library.

ISBN: 1 903499 08 9 (Paperback)
ISBN: 1 903499 18 6 (Hardback)

Typeset by Bitter & Twisted. bitter@cybase.co.uk.
Cover design: www.digitaldesign-print.co.uk

Printed and bound in Great Britain by
Lightning Source UK limited, Milton Keynes.

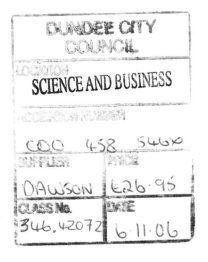

Contents

Preface

All purchasing activities take place within a context of legal regulation, a context that has been taking on increasing importance in recent years. There are a number of reasons for this development. Our involvement in the European Union has resulted in a steady flow of Regulations and Directives imposing additional rules and procedures relating to such issues as tenders, anti-competitive practices, transfer of undertakings, electronic trading and intellectual property rights. There is also a culture change within the UK that has resulted in consumers and businesses becoming increasingly aware of their legal rights and entitlements. It has therefore never been more important for purchasing practitioners to have a basic understanding of the major legal issues and principles that impact on their work. This book is an attempt to provide a clear and concise account of the underlying legal principles which affect the purchasing function.

It is also a useful revision book for candidates studying for the compulsory Legal Aspects for Purchasing & Supply paper at CIPS Professional Stage of the Graduate Diploma. It covers the essential legal themes in a way that focuses on common examination topics. It also develops Competition Law and Intellectual Property Rights in more detail than is usually found in general works on commercial and business law. The book provides practical guidance on examination technique, especially relating to answering legal case studies. Advice on the approach to the study and revision of case law is also featured.

Ian Longdin

January 2005

Table of Cases

Table of Statutes

TABLE OF STATUTORY INSTRUMENTS

TABLE OF EUROPEAN COMMUNITY LEGISLATION

INTERNATIONAL CONVENTIONS AND TREATIES

Chapter 1
Contract Formation

The purpose of this opening chapter is to provide you with a basic understanding of the requirements of a valid contract. It contains a description of the following issues:

- Definition of contract
- Distinctions between deeds and simple contracts
- Essentials of a simple contract
- Distinctions between void, voidable & unenforceable contracts
- Issues relating to letters of intent and comfort.

Contracts form a major part of any organisation's business activities. They will have to be negotiated on a wide range of matters including :

- initial purchase of premises (or lease)
- purchase of raw materials, plant and machinery
- purchase of stock prior to resale
- employment of labour
- sale of goods or services involved.

A contract is defined as a legally binding agreement (enforceable in a court of law).

Form

Contracts are classified into two categories:

- Deeds
- Simple Contracts.

The former are exceptional but are required in certain situations e.g. transferring ownership of land. Sometimes they are used in order to give an agreement a degree of gravity and respectability which can impress on the parties the significance of the situation. (e.g. a partnership agreement; high value contracts between commercial undertakings). They must state on the face of the document that they are deeds and be signed and witnessed to be effective. Another situation where a deed is required is when a gift is being made the subject of a binding and enforceable agreement. Traditionally, local authorities entered into contracts by deed. Although this is no longer required in most cases, the practice does continue but to a far smaller extent. One benefit of entering into a contract by deed is that the ability to sue for breach lasts for 12 years, unlike simple contracts where the limitation period lasts for only six years.

Simple contracts constitute by far the most important category of contract. Almost all commercial and consumer transactions are made in this form. The word "simple" denotes the ease by which such contracts can be made e.g. in written form, by word of mouth, by a combination of the two, or by implication (the conduct of the parties implying a contract has been made). There are a few exceptions where the law insists on the contract being made in written form e.g. consumer credit transactions, contracts for the sale or other disposition of land, contracts of marine insurance.

Essentials of a Simple Contract

Such contracts must satisfy the following requirements in order to be valid:-

- The unconditional acceptance of an offer.

- The presence of "consideration" (a bargain; both parties gaining and losing from the transaction.

- An intention to enter into serious legal relations.

- Contractual capacity ("persons" with limited capacity include registered companies, minors and those registered as of unsound mind).

- Legality of objects (illegal contracts such as cartels in restraint of trade are not enforceable in a court).

- The absence of any "vitiating factors" (See below).

Defective Contracts

If any of the above requirements are not satisfied, the contract will be defective. There are three varieties of defective contract:-

Void Contracts

These are destitute of all legal effect, and cannot be enforced under any circumstances. The parties must be returned to the original position as if no contract had been made at all. Goods must be returned as well as any money already handed over.

The following "vitiating factors" will cause a contract to be declared void:-

- illegality
- fundamental mistake
- absence of consideration.

Voidable Contracts

These are defective but give the "innocent party" an option either to put an end to the contract (to rescind it) or continue and enforce rights under it if necessary.

The following "vitiating factors" cause a contract to be declared voidable:-

- duress
- undue influence
- misrepresentation.

Unenforceable Contracts

These are valid contracts but ones which cannot be enforced because of some technical defect. An example would be the absence of a signed agreement containing specific information as required by the Consumer Credit Act 1974 where a regulated credit agreement is involved. There are not many such examples today.

Letters of Intent and Comfort

Letters of intent often lack the essential of serious legal intent. Examples are letters from a prospective purchaser to a prospective contractor indicating that it is his intention to place a contract with him in the near future. On strict legal analysis, it will be difficult to use a letter of intent as a basis of complaint in court. It will depend critically on the wording found in the letter. If it simply states "We are pleased to inform you that we intend placing an order with you in the near future", the letter will lack serious legal intent. If its wording amounts to a clear acceptance, the fact that it is headed 'Letter of Intent' will not prevent it becoming a binding contract. The most difficult scenario involves a letter expressing an intention to contract coupled with a requirement that the contractor begins to purchase materials or commence work. Here, it can be argued that we are looking at an 'instruction to proceed' – a document authorising the undertaking of expenditure. If, however, this document does not specifically refer to reimbursement, there could still be significant difficulties in claiming the return of monies spent or payment for work carried out.

British Steel Corporation v Cleveland Bridge & Engineering Co Ltd. is an authority illustrating the problems of claiming under a letter of intent.

British Steel Corporation v Cleveland Bridge & Engineering Co Ltd

BSC were negotiating a contract for the sale of steel nodes to be used by CBE on a construction project. CBE had failed to agree on a range of terms and conditions including the price to be paid. However, a letter of intent was received by BSC asking it to commence work on the manufacture of the nodes. This was done and delivery of all the nodes eventually took place whilst the two undertakings continued to negotiate. When BSC brought an action for non-payment it was held that no contract existed and it was not entitled to sue for breach, despite the letter of intent. It was decided, however, that a claim for quantum meruit (as much as is deserved) was available. This entitles a business to claim a reasonable amount for work carried out in circumstances where it was reasonable to expect payment.

Where a contract has been subsequently agreed, there is authority to say that payment for work done prior to agreement will be on the basis of what was agreed in the contract i.e. it will operate retrospectively and cover the earlier period of work undertaken as a result of a letter of intent. This prevents the contractor from bringing a quantum meruit claim which might result in a higher payment figure in some cases (*Trollope & Colls Ltd v Atomic Energy Constructions Ltd*).

Similarly, letters of comfort lack legal enforceability. These represent assurances from a holding company or other subsidiary within a corporate group that contracts being negotiated by one of its subsidiaries (often relating to the seeking of loans) will be honoured and performed satisfactorily. Again, although poor practice, the holding company could not be taken to court if the contract was broken by the subsidiary and it refused to honour the agreement.

Vagueness

It is common to find negotiators unwilling to commit themselves to complete and precise expression of the resulting contractual obligations. This could be caution based on a desire to keep one's options open – avoiding firm commitments which take away flexibility. It could be simply an assumption that where the two businesses have been in regular dealings with each other, there is no need to dot the 'i's and cross the 't's with every new transaction. There is however a danger that if the agreement lacks sufficient coherence it will be regarded as lacking certainty and declared void. Although the courts will look to previous courses of dealing and widely known national conditions of contract (found in some standard forms of contract), there is a limit to such a willingness to find the missing elements. The courts will not construct a contract on behalf of the parties.

King's Motors (Oxford) Ltd v Lax

A lease contained an option for a further period of years 'at such rental as may be agreed upon between the parties'. When the tenant attempted to exercise this option the landlord gave notice of termination, claiming the option lacked certainty and was therefore void.

HELD: In the absence of an arbitration clause allowing for a procedure to quantify the new rental, it was void through lack of certainty.

In Conclusion

- A contract is a legally binding agreement, enforceable in a court of law
- The great majority of contracts are classified as 'simple', meaning there is a flexibility as to how they can be created – they do not have to be in writing
- Unlike deeds, simple contracts require the presence of 'consideration', and have a limitation period of 6 years instead of 12 years
- If any of the essentials of a simple contract are missing, the contract is defective
- Void contracts are so fundamentally flawed that the court will never permit rights or duties to be enforceable – they are a nullity – of no legal effect whatsoever
- Voidable contracts, although defective, can be enforced by the innocent party if it opts to do so. Alternatively, it can opt to rescind (cancel) the contract
- Letters of intent and letters of comfort often lack the essential of intention to enter into legal relations. However, it is vital to examine the precise wording before a conclusion can be drawn
- Agreements can be declared invalid for a lack of clarity where aspects of the agreement are considered too vague (the rules of offer and acceptance having been improperly observed).

Chapter 2
Offer and Acceptance

We now need to examine the technical rules of offer and acceptance. This provides a background in order to study such practical issues as the battle of the forms and the tender process. The chapter contains a discussion of the following legal principles:

- Definition of offer
- Distinction between offer and invitation to treat
- Termination of offer
- Requirements for a valid acceptance
- Communication of acceptance .

All agreements must contain an offer by one person which has been accepted by another (or group of persons)
A body of legal rules has been drawn up over the last century which is intended to make sure that all contracts contain clear, definite commitments and have been specifically agreed beyond doubt.

Business negotiators prefer to deal with each other on a more flexible basis often making much looser arrangements which can be modified or added to at a later stage. This approach can backfire if the agreement becomes the subject of a legal action in court and is declared of no legal effect giving no legal rights to either party.

Offer and Acceptance
Basic Legal Requirements

Offer

An offer is a clear, specific commitment to be legally bound to a proposal simply by its acceptance.

[The word 'offer' will often not be used in practice – alternatives such as proposal, bid and tender will be far more common]

An offer must be distinguished from other statements made during contractual preliminaries. (**invitations to treat**) The latter do not normally produce legal commitments or obligations – they are merely concerned with information requesting or providing. Only a firm offer, clearly indicating that the offeror intends to be bound without further negotiations, is capable of acceptance so that a binding contract is achieved.

The following situations have been held to be invitations to treat, not offers. In each case the reason is practical rather than strictly arrived at by logic.

Displays of Goods for Sale

These are considered to be invitations for offers to be made by the customer.

This protects the shop if a wrong price has been placed on the item involved.

Fisher v Bell

A shopkeeper was prosecuted for 'offering' offensive weapons for sale, by having flick-knives on display in his window.

HELD: Technically, he was not offering the goods for sale – he was inviting offers from customers. He had to be acquitted.

[The legislation was amended to make 'displaying goods for purposes of sale' also an offence]

Advertisements, Circulars, Price Lists and Catalogues

These are usually held to be invitations for offers to be made by the potential buyers. Sometimes the reason is "best price" opportunity (adverts); sometimes it is to prevent difficulties relating to shortage of stock (catalogues, circulars)

Websites

Almost all websites are regarded as invitations to treat, encouraging visitors to the site to offer to buy the goods involved.

Auctions

The auctioneer is said to be inviting offers from members in the audience. This enables him to accept the highest offer.

N.B. Tenders submitted by outside contractors are regarded as offers. The original proposal requesting for tenders to be submitted is an invitation for offers to be made (enabling the firm receiving the tenders to pick the best bid).

Offers must be clear and specific, not vague.

Offers can be accepted at any time until they terminate.

Termination of offer can occur by:-

- Revocation (withdrawal)

- Rejection (including counter-offer)

    By its rejection, the offer automatically ceases to exist. The same result occurs when a counter offer is made – it is as if the person making the counter offer had rejected the first offer, even if he uses words suggesting acceptance ("Your offer is accepted (if) ...").

- Lapse of time

    An offer will lapse either at the end of a specified time if one was attached to the offer (seven days, 28 days) or a reasonable period of time where none is specified. What is reasonable depends on the circumstances of each case – the nature of the goods, the context in which the offer was sent etc.

- Failure of a condition precedent

  An example would be an offer to sell goods, subject to obtaining the necessary export licence. If the licence is not granted, the offer would terminate.

- Death of the offeror(the person making the offer)

Acceptance

Acceptance of an Offer must be Unqualified

The only legitimate way to accept an offer is to do so unconditionally, without provisos, or amendments or additions. Where the latter are involved it is considered, in law, to be a rejection of the original offer. (although in business practice it is seen more in terms of feeling one's way to an eventual agreement).

Such conditional acceptances are regarded in law as counter offers still requiring acceptance by the other party.

Hyde v Wrench

The defendant offered his farm to the claimant for £1000. The claimant replied offering £950. The defendant subsequently rejected this, so the claimant purported to accept the original £1000 offer. It was held that there was no contract since the original offer had been extinguished by the counter offer. Although expressed as an acceptance, it was in fact a fresh offer.

One example of this principle is seen in the clause "subject to contract". Although most frequently seen in connection with house sales it can apply to any business contract. Its effect is to ensure that the parties are not bound until a formal contract is drawn up and signed. This provides a breathing space in which to check on certain matters in the meantime e.g. finance, surveys etc.

The reason why the agreement is not yet binding is because the offer was accepted with conditions - "subject to contract" and was not therefore a proper acceptance. [Requests for clarification and further information do not amount to counter offer though.]

Acceptance must be Communicated to the Offeror (by Words or Conduct)

Silence cannot be taken to mean acceptance e.g. "If I don't hear from you in the next week, I'll take it that you've accepted my offer".

Felthouse v Bindley

An uncle wrote to his nephew offering to buy the nephew's horse for £30. 15s. and stating "If I don't hear any more about him I shall consider the horse mine at that price". The nephew gave instructions to the defendant, an auctioneer, not to sell the horse as he intended it for his uncle. The defendant inadvertently sold the horse, and the uncle sued him in the tort of conversion. **HELD:** The horse had not become the uncle's property – no contract had been concluded. There had been no communication of acceptance to the uncle.

Acceptance Can be Implied by Conduct

Brogden v Metropolitan Railway Co

The railway company had been supplied with coal from Brogden for many years. The company was keen to have a formal agreement. It drew up a draft agreement, which was sent to Brogden, and was returned by him to the company marked "approved", although he had inserted a new term to the draft. For the next two years coal was supplied and paid for between the parties in accordance with the draft agreement, although the company never gave notification that they had accepted it. In fact over the two years it lay in a desk drawer. Then a dispute arose between the parties. Brogden alleged that there was no contract binding them. The House of Lords disagreed, taking the view that there was a contract, based on conduct. This occurred when the order was placed for the coal on the terms of the draft agreement, although it had never been formally accepted.

When is Acceptance Effective?

Normally acceptance is effective from the moment when the communication is received by the offeree. This applies to instantaneous methods of communication, which includes acceptances by fax. Failure in the transmission of a fax containing an acceptance therefore means no contract has been concluded – even though it was sent, it was not received. The position regarding emails is less clear cut, partly because it is unclear whether it amounts to instantaneous communication or delayed communication. It is also affected by whether a common server is used by both organisations or separate servers(!).

Acceptance communicated through the post is an exception.

The Postal Rule

Where the post is the recognised medium of communication the acceptance is complete as soon as it is properly put in the post.
The rules as to postal communications apply similarly to telegrams.

In other words, one set of rules apply to instant delivery methods of communication e.g. phone, telex, face to face; another set of rules apply to delayed communications e.g. post, telegrams. The postal rule of acceptance can be overridden if the offer specifically states that acceptance will not be effective until received e.g. upon notification of acceptance.

In Conclusion

- An offer is a clear, specific commitment to be bound by a proposal – all that is required is an acceptance for it to be transformed into a binding contract

- Words used in lieu of 'offer' include bid, proposal, price and tender

- An invitation to treat is a preliminary stage prior to an offer being made – where a party is encouraging an offer from the other party

- Classic examples of invitation to treat are circulars, price lists, most advertisements, requests for tenders, auctions and goods on display in shops

- Offers terminate in a number of ways, including revocation (withdrawal), rejection (including counter offer) and lapse of time

- Acceptance must be unqualified, otherwise it is a rejection (by counter offer)

- Acceptance must be positively communicated – silence is not enough

- Acceptance is effective only when received if an instantaneous method of communication is used

- Acceptance is effective as soon as it is sent (posted) if a delayed method of communication is used

Chapter 3
Practical Applications

The Battle of the Forms

The next chapter concentrates on the issues relating to whose set of terms will govern the contract – those of the buyer or supplier. This topic involves a direct application of the rules of offer and acceptance discussed in Chapter Two. It will therefore be important to have read and understood the earlier material. This chapter includes discussion of the following principles and issues:

- Meaning and significance of standard form contracts
- Why important to win the battle of the forms
- Legal analysis of documentation stage
- Landmark cases

It is normal business practice at the negotiation stage for both the buyer and the seller to utilise pre-printed contractual documentation – their standard terms of purchase or supply. Agreements reached on the basis of these documents are known as standard form contracts. It saves time in concluding contracts and allows central management to control the specific terms and conditions being agreed by their staff at different locations.

It is obvious that these standard terms will be drafted in ways that are favourable to the purchaser or seller in question. Examples of how the pre-printed terms can vary include:

- Termination and cancellation rights of the buyer for late delivery
- Price (whether fixed or variable)
- Risk liability (for accidental loss or damage)
- Passing of ownership (whether on delivery or retained until payment)
- Exclusion of liability.

For these reasons (and others) it is important for the buyer to successfully impose its terms over those of the seller – to win the battle of the forms. Let us take a typical sequence of events leading up to the conclusion of a contract:

What do each of these stages represent in the language of offer and acceptance?

Stage One	Invitation to treat
Stage Two	Offer (in most cases)
Stage Three	Counter offer (changing the terms which apply)
Stage Four	Counter offer (again, changing the terms).

This could be the conclusion of any correspondence between the parties. The fact that the buyer does not reply to the acknowledgement note cannot be taken to be acceptance of this last counter-offer - silence is not sufficient (*Felthouse v Bindley*).

In practice, delivery is often the next event. If the buyer receives delivery of the relevant goods, his conduct (in allowing the delivery to take place) will be taken to be implied acceptance of the counter-offer (*Brogden v Metropolitan Rly Co*). This may be further reinforced by signing the seller's delivery documentation which could refer to conditions of sale again. In such a case, the seller's terms will govern the contract. In the words of Lord Denning, the battle of the forms is won by the party who 'fires the last shot.' This normally favours the seller whose acknowledgement note is often the last document to be sent.

What then can the buyer do? Initial correspondence (such as general enquiries) should refer to conditions of purchase governing the contract, as should the order form when submitted (it is usual to include a term insisting that 'our terms shall prevail' over any others which may be subsequently introduced. The case of *Butler Machine Tool Co. Ltd v Ex Cell O Ltd* makes clear that such assertions do not bring victory as they are contained on documents which cease to be effective once rejected by a counter offer.) The buyer should include a tear-off slip to be returned with acceptance of the order – the slip confirming that the contract is to be concluded on the buyer's terms. If the seller fails to return the slip (and returns an acknowledgement note referring to seller's terms) the buyer should reply and require acceptance on buyer's terms only. At this juncture, market forces (or a combination of ignorance and/or inertia) will decide who is successful.

The two leading cases which illustrate the battle of the forms are *Butler Machine Tool Co. Ltd v Ex Cell O Ltd* and *BRS Ltd v Arthur Crutchley Ltd.*

Butler Machine Tool v Ex-cell-o Corporation (1979)

Negotiations took place for the purchase of some heavy machinery. A quotation was sent which included a delivery date and price - £75,500). On the back of the quote it stated :-

"All orders accepted only upon and subject to the terms set out in our quotation and the following conditions. These terms shall prevail over any terms in the buyer's order."

The terms included a price variation clause.
The buyer submitted an order for the purchase of the machinery which included the following wording :-

"Please supply on terms and conditions as below and overleaf".

These terms stipulated a fixed price. The order had a tear off slip (acknowledgement) to be returned stating :-

"We accept your order on the terms and conditions stated thereon".

The acknowledgement slip was duly signed but a covering letter was also sent stating :-

"This is being entered in accordance with our revised quotation of the 23 May".

A dispute then arose concerning the price to be paid. Whose terms govern the contract?

Held: The buyer's terms governed the contract. The return of the buyer's acknowledgement slip was the critical issue. The accompanying letter was not worded in strong enough language to suggest a re-imposition of the seller's terms. It simply confirmed the original details relating to price and identity of the machine.

(The position would not have been clear if such strong language had been used in the covering letter – or a copy of the seller's acknowledgement note referring to the seller's conditions had been included with the buyer's acknowledgement slip. It can be argued that such a reply causes so much uncertainty that no agreement has been made and that it does not even amount to a counter-offer. Remember, offers must consist of clear, specific commitments. There is no authority for this particular scenario and it is possible that a court could rule the buyer's slip to be effective and not negated by the accompanying material.

BRS v Arthur Crutchley Ltd

A road haulage company "agreed" a contract to deliver a consignment of whisky to a wholesaler (CrutchleyLtd). During the negotiations various documents (conditions of carriage; conditions of supply) had been referred to but never confirmed. The driver for the haulage company arrived at the gates of the wholesale company and handed the warehouse manager a delivery note (incorporating their conditions of carriage). The note was stamped by the manager "received under Crutchley's conditions". The whisky was taken off the lorry and stored in the warehouse. A dispute subsequently occurred and it was necessary to know whose conditions governed the contract.

Held: By stamping the note, Crutchley's manager had made a counter offer which was accepted by implication – the conduct of the driver (acting as agent for BRS), in allowing the goods to be taken off his lorry, amounting to an acceptance of this counter offer. Consequently, Crutchley's terms governed the contract.

In Conclusion

- Standard form contracts (pre-printed, containing identical terms for all customers/suppliers) comprise the basis of most business transactions

- Each party's terms are drafted in ways favourable to its own position – hence the need to win the battle of the forms

- Each attempt to change the basis of the contract from one set of terms to another set is technically a counter offer and therefore a rejection of the previous offer

- The battle is usually won by 'he who fires the last shot' – the party who submits the final document stating that its terms will govern the contract

- The contract may not strictly be agreed until delivery, when receiving the goods may be treated as implied acceptance of the terms submitted in the supplier's acknowledgement note

Chapter 4
Consideration and Duress

This chapter focuses on some of the more practical issues relating to two of the essentials of a simple contract outlined in Chapter One – the need for consideration and consent to be present in the transaction. It covers the following legal principles:

- Consideration – basic definition
- Adequacy of consideration
- Consideration must be new and additional
- Duress – basic definitions (including economic duress)
- Landmark cases.

Consideration

All simple contracts require consideration. This means the presence of a bargain. Both parties must be seen to sacrifice something in return for the benefit obtained. There must be a give and take - an exchange. It need not be adequate. The courts will not come to the rescue of a person who has made a bad bargain - unless there is some further element of undue pressure or misrepresentation involved.

The sacrifice must be something new and additional to any existing commitments or obligations though. Merely promising again to perform an existing obligation is not valid consideration.

Compare: *Stilk v Myrick*
             Hartley v Ponsonby

In the former case, a ship's crew was promised an extra £10 each if they agreed to sail the ship home light-handed (two of the crew had deserted). When they were not paid at the end of the voyage they sued for breach of contract. The court held that in effect they were doing nothing more in substance than they were already obliged to do under their existing contract. They lost their claim.

In the Hartley case, a similar promise was made but in a situation where half the crew had deserted. In this case the claims were successful. The court decided that the new arrangement was substantially different to the initial agreement and involved serious safety hazards. New consideration had therefore been provided.

A more recent case of importance is *Atlas Express Ltd v Kafco Ltd.* Kafco were heavily dependent on a contract to supply basketware to Woolworths. Atlas were aware of this. A contract price for delivering the goods to Woolworths had been agreed by Atlas, who were road hauliers. It had been made on the assumption that the lorries would be fully loaded which in practice turned out not to be the case - they were often half empty. Subsequently, Atlas insisted on an increase in their charges at short notice and in a way which clearly jeopardised Kafco's future relations with Woolworths. Reluctantly, Kafco agreed but later refused to pay the increase. The court held that the claim for breach of contract had to fail for

- there had been no consideration by Atlas - they were doing nothing more than they were already obliged to do under the existing contract
- their threat (not to deliver the goods) amounted to economic duress (see below)

A very controversial case in this area is *Williams & Co v Roffey Bros.* Roffey had contracted to refurbish a block of flats. They had subcontracted the joinery work to Williams for a price of £20,000. Roffey became aware of financial problems that Williams were getting into and the fact that they would not complete the joinery work on schedule. This would result in Roffey being hit by substantial liquidated damages for late completion of the refurbishment. Roffey therefore offered to pay Williams an additional sum for each flat completed. At the end of the work they refused to pay this extra money and were sued for breach of contract. The court held that:-

- Consideration had been provided by Williams in that the new arrangement had enabled Roffey to avoid paying the liquidated damages which would otherwise have been payable.

- There had been no economic duress involved - Roffey had been the party to suggest making the payment and therefore there had been no coercion.

Accordingly, Williams' claim for breach of contract was successful and they were entitled to the extra payments.

Duress

A contract will be voidable if one of the parties was coerced into making the agreement. This can be either the result of physical threats (presumably not too common in business circles) or threats affecting the economic position of the business. A clear example of the latter is the case discussed above - *Atlas Express Ltd v Kafco Ltd.*
Another case illustrating the principle is *North Ocean Shipping Co. v Hyundai Construction (The Atlantic Baron).* A contract had been agreed for the building of a ship. Whilst the ship was being built, the builders insisted on an additional 10% on the price. Without the ship, the buyers would have lost a profitable contract for the charter of the vessel. The buyers paid the additional money and then sued for its recovery, arguing economic duress. The court decided that the actions of the builders constituted economic duress but, because the buyers had delayed bringing their claim, they had affirmed the new arrangement and were obliged to pay the extra money.

There is clearly a very fine line to be drawn between the normal cut and thrust of commercial bargaining and unfairly forcing a party to agree to terms without the necessary element of consent. Each case will have to be considered on its own merits and the ability to predict court decisions will be inevitably extremely difficult.

In Conclusion

- Consideration is the presence of a sacrifice in exchange for a benefit from both parties

- Consideration does not have to be adequate (unless misrepresentation or duress is involved)

- Consideration must involve the sacrifice of something new and additional – using existing obligations is not a valid basis for obtaining new benefits

- Duress involves coercion – the forcing of a person into a contract against his will

- Economic duress operates where knowledge of an organisation's economic needs is used to its detriment in an unfair manner by insisting that it enters into an unfavourable contract

Chapter 5
Major Vitiating Factors

Mistake
Misrepresentation

We are still examining the essentials of a valid contract. In the last chapter, we saw that the required consent (genuine agreement) was lacking if the agreement was made under duress. In this chapter, it will become apparent that certain types of mistake can invalidate agreements. Additionally, where a party has been misled in a way which amounts to misrepresentation, the resulting agreement can be declared invalid. Damages may also be available. In both these cases, the defect relates to the lack of genuine consent obtained. This chapter covers the following legal principles:

- Mistake – normal position (caveat emptor)
- Exceptions – types of operative mistake
- Misrepresentation – definition
- Distinction from traders' puff and contractual terms
- Remedies for misrepresentation

Mistake

The usual approach of the courts where one or both parties have made a mistake is to insist that the contract must stand. The courts will not come to the protection of parties who have made a bad bargain (Caveat Emptor

- Let the Buyer Beware). This maxim applies in fact to both parties - the seller as well as the buyer. However, in a few exceptional situations the courts will declare a contract to be void for "operative" or "fundamental" mistake:-

■ **Common Mistake as to the Existence of the Subject-Matter** e.g. agreeing to buy/sell specific goods which have already been destroyed at the time of the agreement. (The Sale of Goods Act 1979 recognises this exception in section 7)

Scott v Coulson

G. agreed to assign to H an assurance policy on the life of L. L. had died before the agreement was made. **Held:** There was no contract

■ **Mutual Mistake** - where the two parties have been completely at cross purposes from the very start and have never been agreeing to the same deal at all.

Raffles v Wichelhaus

An agreement was made by which a quantity of cotton was to arrive "ex Peerless from Bombay". There were two SS Peerless vessels sailing from Bombay – the defendant intended the one arriving in October; the claimant intended the one arriving in December. **Held:** The court was unable to decide which party had formed the correct interpretation. The contract was therefore declared void.

■ **Mistake as to the Identity of the Other party (Unilateral Mistake)** - this exception normally involves one party attempting to commit fraud on the other by pretending to be some other person or firm. It will not usually apply where the two parties are dealing with each other face to face - it is argued that misrepresentation is the appropriate vitiating factor in this situation.

■ **Non Est Factum ("It is not my Deed")** i.e. the person who signed the contract did not realise the nature of the contract being entered into. It is extremely difficult to use this defence successfully because you have to prove that:

- you mistook the type of agreement involved (not just its contents or detail), and

- you were not negligent in doing so (something which in practice may be quite difficult to prove.)

Saunders v Anglia Building Society

Mrs. Gallie, a 78 year-old widow, signed a document without reading it – her glasses were broken at the time. She had been assured by a friend of her nephew that it was a deed of gift to her nephew. In fact it was a deed of gift to the friend. Soon after he mortgaged the property to the building society. Mrs. Gallie argued that the contract was void through non est factum. **Held:** Her action failed because, although it was accepted that she had not been careless, the document was not fundamentally different to the one she intended to sign.

Occasionally, the courts will operate the remedy of **rectification** where a document has been completed in error and does not represent the true wishes of the parties. Rather than declaring the entire agreement to be void, the court amends the document to bring it into line with the original wishes of the two parties e.g. where a typographical error has been made and not discovered on proofreading.

Joscelyne v Nissen

The claimant agreed to transfer his car-hire business to his daughter in return for her agreeing to pay a number of household expenses. When a written contract was subsequently drawn up it did not mention payment of these expenses. **Held**: The agreement should be rectified to include this commitment.

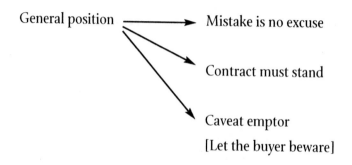

General position → Mistake is no excuse

Contract must stand

Caveat emptor
[Let the buyer beware]

Exceptions (Operative Mistake)

- Common mistake as to the existence of the subject matter
- Mutual mistake
- Mistake as to the identity of the other party
- Non est factum (it is not my deed).

Misrepresentation

If a person has been misled during the preliminary stages leading to a contract, s/he will want to know what rights, if any, s/he possesses. These depend on the nature of the false statement and how it can be classified legally. There are three main types of false statement:-

- Traders' Puff
- Misrepresentation
- Contractual Term.

Traders' Puff

Certain statements made by a trader are regarded as mere "puffs" not intended to have any legal consequences. In *Lambert v Lewis* the manufacturers of a towing hitch claimed in promotional literature that it was "foolproof" and "required no maintenance". One hitch which was sold with a defect caused a serious accident. The Court of Appeal held that the promotional claims were not intended to be serious promises which gave rise to any contractual rights in themselves.

Misrepresentation

A misrepresentation may be defined as a false statement of fact which induces the other party to enter into a contract. It must be a statement of fact, not future intention (unless it can be proved that at the time of the false statement, the person making it must not have believed in its accuracy). It must also induce (or at least partly induce) the other party to enter into the contract. If s/he knew it was untrue or did not believe in its truth and yet went ahead with the deal it did not act as an inducement.

Misrepresentations differ from contractual terms in that they remain outside the contract once it has been agreed. In other words, they influence a party to enter into the agreement but, in the circumstances, are not seen to be a part of the actual contract. Remedies for misrepresentation are therefore not strictly contractual – they arise through a combination of statutory rights and use of the law of tort

Remedies for Misrepresentation

This will depend on the type of misrepresentation. There are three categories:

- Fraudulent
- Negligent
- Wholly innocent.

Fraudulent

A misstatement is made fraudulently if it is made knowingly, or without belief in its truth, or recklessly, careless whether it be true of false. Fraud is very difficult to prove in practice.
The innocent party can claim :-

- Rescission of the contract (but see below - loss of right to rescind)
- Damages for the tort of deceit.

Negligent

A false statement of fact will be deemed to have been made negligently unless the party making the statement "proves that he had reasonable ground to believe and did believe up to the time the contract was made that the facts were true [Section 2(1) Misrepresentation Act 1967]. The burden of proof is on the trader to disprove negligence.

The innocent party can claim :-

- Rescission of the contract (unless the judge uses his discretion to award damages in lieu) [Section 2(1)]

- Damages.

N.B. It will not be possible under Section 2(1) of the Misrepresentation Act 1967 to claim rights if you did not enter into a contract with the maker of the false statement, but have nevertheless suffered financial loss as a result e.g. a house purchaser who relies on the report of a valuer acting for the building society. It may be possible to bring a claim for negligence (a tort action) using the precedent of *Hedley Byrne & Co v Heller & Partners* (1964). If a special relationship exists between the maker of a false statement and another (usually where the former is in a professional position and whose judgement will be relied upon to a high degree) s/he owes the latter a duty of care and can be liable for damage (including economic loss) caused by a breach of duty.

Wholly Innocent

Section 2(2) Misrepresentation Act 1967 entitles the innocent party to :

- Rescission of the contract (unless the judge uses discretion to award damages in lieu).

Loss of Right to Rescind

- where the innocent party has already affirmed the contract
- where the judge uses discretion and awards damages in lieu
- if an innocent third party has acquired rights to the goods already

- if it has become impossible to restore the original position e.g. the goods have been altered in their appearance
- lapse of time (after reasonable length of time) – at some point the other party should be entitled to feel secure that the contract must stand.

Leaf v International Galleries

The claimant bought a painting in 1944, relying on a statement by the defendant that it was painted by Constable. In 1949 he discovered it was an imitation and worth much less. He brought an action for rescission of the contract and the return of his purchase price. **HELD**: It was too late for such a claim – a reasonable period of time had already elapsed and he had now accepted the painting.

There is a degree of overlap between pre-contractual statements that constitute misrepresentations and those amounting to contractual terms. Sometimes, the court has elevated a misrepresentation to the status of a contractual term:

Esso Petroleum Co Ltd v Mardon

An over-optimistic sales forecast made by a senior sales executive of Esso (that the throughput of a filling station would amount to 200,000 gallons per year) was held to constitute a breach of contract – the statement amounting to a warranty. This was the case even though it had not been included in the specific terms written into the contract.

Misrepresentation

Fraudulent   made knowingly, or recklessly

Negligent   honest belief, but with no
                  reasonable grounds

Innocent   honest belief, and with reasonable grounds

Fraudulent Yes   Yes – tort claim
                                             for deceit

Negligent   Yes   Yes, either:

                                             a) statutory claim
                                             under s.2.1

                                             Misrepresentation Act
                                             1967,or

                                             b) tort claim in

                                             negligence (Hedley

                                             Byrne v Heller &
                                             Partners)

Innocent   Yes   No, unless judge uses
                                             discretion to award
                                             damages in lieu (s.2.2)

In conclusion

■ Mistakes do not usually affect the validity of a contract (Caveat Emptor
  – Let the buyer beware).

■ Operative mistakes are the exceptions – ones which are so
  fundamental that it is as if no agreement has been made at all

■ The main examples of operative mistake are common mistake as to the
  existence of the subject-matter, mutual mistake, mistake as to the
  identity of the other party and non est factum ('it is not my deed')

■ The court may rectify (correct) a document where its wording, by
  oversight, does not reflect the true intentions of the parties

■ Misrepresentation is a false statement of fact which induces the other
  party to enter into a contract

■ Remedies for misrepresentation are not contractual – by definition,
  the misrepresentation has not been incorporated as a term in the
  contract

■ Rescission (avoidance) of the contract is nearly always available

■ The availability of damages as a remedy depends on whether the
  misrepresentation was committed fraudulently, negligently or
  innocently.

Chapter 6
The Contents
of a Contract

Contractual Terms

So far we have been examining issues connected with formation of contract and whether contracts will be invalid for one reason or another. The next chapter focuses on the substance of a contract – what it actually contains. Its terms can be classified in a number of ways and the following material introduces you to the topic. Breach of contract and available remedies play a central part in this discussion. The chapter covers the following issues:

- Terms – classification according to manner of creation
- Terms – classification according to importance (conditions, warranties, innominate)
- Remedies for breach
- Acceptance of goods – effect on right of buyer to repudiate.

Most business transactions contain a combination of basic obligations and ones that are less significant. The make of a washing machine, for instance, as well as its colour, price, and date of delivery are all detailed provisions of how the contract is to be performed. These details are known as the terms of the contract. All contracts contain such terms. They comprise the more specific detailed undertakings of how the basic obligations are to be performed. In a contract for the construction of a new factory building, the start and completion dates, the design of the building, the materials to be used, the extent to which work can be subcontracted etc are all integral parts of the contract and are all equally enforceable.

Terms can be classified in two different ways:

- according to their manner of creation
- according to their importance to the contract.

Manner of Creation

Express Terms - These are the details of the contract that have been specifically and mutually agreed upon before or at the time the contract is made.

They are intended by the parties to form part of the contract. They can be made orally, or they can be reduced to writing.

The problem here is that not everything said in the negotiations to an agreement forms an integral part of it. Express terms must be distinguished from mere representations (statements made prior to the agreement, at the negotiation stage, which induce one party to enter into the contract but do not form part of it). If the statement made turns out to be false, even if made innocently or negligently, then this will amount to misrepresentation and damages can now be paid under the Misrepresentation Act 1967.

Implied Terms - Terms will sometimes be attached to contracts by operation of law. This will add terms which the law either thinks fitting and appropriate to include in the agreement or need to be added in order to give the contract the business effect intended by the parties.

Attachment can be by :

- Act of Parliament
- common law
- commercial custom.

Importance to the Contract

Condition - A major term of the contract; one that is so vital that, if it is broken, it renders performance of the contract fundamentally different from that which had originally been envisaged. e.g. if you had continuously stressed the importance of a particular completion date to a supplier and it fails to deliver or complete on time, it is highly probable that the courts would interpret this as a breach of a condition.

Warranty - A minor term of the contract; one that is not so vital that breach of it results in a totally different contract. It is a subsidiary term which merely adds the details to other more important terms.

The importance of the distinction between a condition and a warranty will become obvious when it is related to the area of remedies for breach of contract. If a condition of the contract is broken, then fairly serious and drastic remedies will be available against the party in breach. The injured party can repudiate the contract (terminate it) and claim damages, or he may continue with the contract and claim damages.

If a warranty of the contract is broken, however, then the remedies available will not be so far-reaching; the injured party must continue with the contract, and only claim damages

You might well be a little confused by the choice of wording used here. Written contracts often contain the heading "Terms and Conditions." This is mere terminology as they will contain both conditions and warranties as defined above. Equally, the expression "warranty" is often used to mean a form of guarantee when purchasing goods. This is simply another use of the word and is not relevant to the classification of terms in a contract.

How to Determine Whether Condition or Warranty

It may be self evident in the situation e.g. completion of construction work to meet a known deadline (the Millennium Dome, facilities for the next Olympics).

It may be specified by law, either in legislation e.g. the implied duties relating to goods found ss 12-15 Sale of Goods Act 1979 are stipulated to be conditions by the Act itself), or common law e.g. an 'expedited readiness to load' clause in a charterparty (contract for carriage of goods by sea) is presumed to be a condition.

Self-Description in the contract, although not conclusive, will be taken into account by the court and influence its decision. In *Lombard North Central plc v Butterworth*, a contract for the lease of a computer involved instalment payments. The contract specified that prompt payments were of the essence. When payment was late the court held that this entitled the supplier to terminate the contract – a condition having been broken. [there is a presumption in sale of goods contracts that time for payment is not a condition – in the absence of other factors].

Contractual Terms

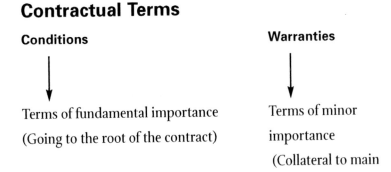

Conditions

Terms of fundamental importance
(Going to the root of the contract)

Warranties

Terms of minor
importance
(Collateral to main
purpose)

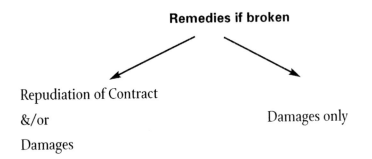

Remedies if broken

Repudiation of Contract
&/or
Damages

Damages only

But check if buyer has "accepted" the goods – see later.

"Innominate Terms"

Traditionally, terms have been divided into two types - conditions and warranties. A condition is a term of major importance; if it is broken, the other party is entitled to treat the contract as at an end as well as claiming damages. A warranty is a less important term; for breach of a warranty the other party may recover damages only, but may not treat the contract as terminated. In other words, if someone has failed to perform a condition in the contract, he has effectively repudiated the contract with the result that the other party is released from his contractual obligations and need not perform either. Sometimes (as we have already seen) it is clear whether a term is a condition or a warranty, eg. when the matter is covered by legislation. The Sale of Goods Act 1979 identifies implied conditions relating to the quality and fitness of goods sold for example. Where a seller breaks such a provision a buyer is entitled to reject the goods, claim a full refund of any money paid, and in addition recover damages, eg. where the goods are defective and the market price of similar goods is higher than the agreed contract price. However, where the provision is an express one, the task is more difficult. Nor is the matter of interpretation of the provisions made easier by the fact that the agreement uses words like "condition" or "warranty", for it may well be that the parties, who are commercial people, not lawyers, have not used the words in a legalistic sense but are using them as synonyms for "provision" or "term". The question to be decided usually is whether the parties intended the term to be an important or fundamental term going to the root of the contract (a condition) or thought it less significant (a warranty).

However, that straightforward division of terms into 2 types was disturbed by the sensible and vitally important decision in 1962 - the *Hong Kong Fir Shipping* case. This case introduced the concept of the innominate term (or intermediate term). This is a term which, when the contract is first made, cannot be put into one of the two traditional pigeon holes as it covers a multitude of possible breaches of small or large significance. So the remedy of the innocent party will depend on the nature, consequences, and effect of the breach ie. whether the term is broken seriously or not. The *Hong Kong Fir* case is a clear illustration. That case was concerned with an obligation of seaworthiness of a ship. The Court of Appeal pointed out that the breaches which might occur were various. They might be extremely trivial - the omission of a nail; they might be extremely grave - a serious defect in the hull or in the machinery. So the Court decided that it was impossible to identify the seaworthiness obligation as a condition; the parties would have to wait to see how, if at all, the term was broken.

Breach of Contract - Loss of Right to Repudiate

Where a condition or major term of a contract is broken by the seller, the buyer's primary remedy, apart from compensation for loss, is the right of rejection - the right to refuse to take delivery or, if the goods have already been delivered, to make the seller collect them, and in addition, to have any advance payment returned by the seller.

This right is lost however where the buyer has "accepted" the goods e.g. made up the raw materials or fitted components into his end product; or kept the goods for an unreasonably long time without rejecting rather than contacting his supplier promptly he finds something wrong.

The relevant provisions are found in the Sale of Goods Act 1979:

SALE OF GOODS ACT 1979

SECTION 11 (4)

WHERE A CONTRACT OF SALE IS NOT SEVERABLE AND THE BUYER HAS ACCEPTED THE GOODS OR PART OF THEM... THE BREACH OF A CONDITION TO BE FULFILLED BY THE SELLER CAN ONLY BE TREATED AS A BREACH OF WARRANTY, AND NOT AS A GROUND FOR REJECTING THE GOODS AND TREATING THE CONTRACT AS REPUDIATED, UNLESS THERE IS AN EXPRESS OR IMPLIED TERM OF THE CONTRACT TO THAT EFFECT.

SECTION 35(2)

WHERE GOODS ARE DELIVERED TO THE BUYER, AND HE HAS NOT PREVIOUSLY EXAMINED THEM, HE IS NOT DEEMED TO HAVE ACCEPTED THEM ... UNTIL HE HAS HAD A REASONABLE OPPORTUNITY OF EXAMINING THEM FOR THE PURPOSE – OF ASCERTAINING WHETHER THEY ARE IN CONFORMITY WITH THE CONTRACT

SECTION 35

(1)(a)   THE BUYER IS DEEMED TO HAVE ACCEPTED THE GOODS:- WHEN HE INTIMATES TO THE SELLER THAT HE HAS ACCEPTED THEM, OR,

(b)   WHEN THE GOODS HAVE BEEN DELIVERED TO HIM AND HE DOES ANY ACT IN RELATION TO THEM WHICH IS INCONSISTENT WITH THE OWNERSHIP OF THE SELLER, OR,

(4)   WHEN AFTER THE LAPSE OF A REASONABLE TIME, HE RETAINS THE GOODS WITHOUT INTIMATING TO THE SELLER THAT HE HAS REJECTED THEM.

In Conclusion

- Contractual terms can be classified according to how they were created (express; implied), or according to their importance to the contract (conditions; warranties)

- Express terms are agreed between the parties; implied terms are automatically incorporated by operation of law (chiefly by statute or common law)

- Conditions are terms of fundamental importance, breach of which entitles the injured party to repudiate (terminate) the contract and/or claim damages

- Warranties are terms of relatively minor importance, breach of which entitles the injured party to claim damages – it cannot repudiate the contract

- Sometimes, it is impossible to determine whether breach of a term entitles the injured party to repudiate the contract until after the breach has taken place and its consequences on the entire contract assessed – these are called innominate terms

- A buyer loses the right to repudiate a contract for breach of a condition once the goods in question have been accepted.

Chapter 7
Remedies for Breach

Liquidated Damages and Penalties

Unliquidated Damages (Damages at Large)

Damages are always available for breach of contract. Sometimes the claimable amount will have been specified in the contract. Sometimes, it will have to be assessed by the court. The following chapter examines the legal principles relevant to the awarding of compensation. It covers the following principles:

- Liquidated damages – definition
- Distinction from penalties
- Advantages of L.D.'s
- Unliquidated damages – underlying purpose
- The Market rule
- The rule in *Hadley v Baxendale*
- Claimable loss
- Proximity of loss to breach
- Mitigation of loss
- Anticipatory breach.

Liquidated Damages

Many contracts include a term providing that specified damages shall be payable in the event of a particular type of breach (usually late delivery or completion of work). There are clear advantages in such a procedure, particularly in avoiding uncertainty and in setting a known limit on the liabilities of the parties. However, a distinction has been made by the courts between liquidated damages clauses and penalty clauses. The significance of this distinction is that the former are enforceable, while the latter are not. This principle is founded on the idea that damages are compensation for loss; a threat designed to compel performance does not qualify as "damages".

The leading case in this area is *Dunlop Pneumatic Tyre Co. Ltd v New Garage & Motor Co. Ltd* (1915). The following principles were laid down in this case.

- The terminology used by the parties is not conclusive. It is a matter of construction for the courts to decide whether a clause is for liquidated damages or a penalty, regardless of how it is described in the contract itself.

- A liquidated damages clause must be a genuine pre-estimate of the actual loss that will be suffered in the event of a breach. The nature of a penalty clause in quite different; it is intended to coerce performance from one of the parties, and a sign of this would be if the amount stipulated is excessive ("extravagant and unconscionable in amount in comparison with the greatest loss that could conceivably be proved to have followed from the breach." - per Lord Dunedin.

- The burden of proof is on the party alleging that the clause is a penalty clause.

- Apart from the criterion already mentioned ("extravagant & unconscionable in amount") another indication that a clause is a penalty is when a single sum is fixed in relation to any possible breach, even though some breaches would clearly cause more loss than others.

- If a clause is construed as liquidated damages, then the amount specified in the clause is what the injured party can recover, regardless of the amount of actual loss:

Cellulose Acetate Silk Co v Widnes Foundry

The defendants had agreed to erect a plant by a specified date. The contract contained a clause requiring them to pay 'by way of penalty' a sum of £20 per week for each week of delay. They were 30 weeks late. The plaintiff claimed their actual losses amounting to £5,850. The defendants relied on the contract provision requiring them to pay only £600. **HELD**: Although called a penalty, the clause was in fact a reasonable attempt to anticipate likely losses and was therefore a liquidated damages clause and effective. The plaintiff was only entitled to £600.

An LD clause should always contain a ceiling or maximum on claimable compensation (e.g. up to a maximum of 5% of the contract price). It is argued that the injured party should have made suitable re-arrangements after a reasonable length of time, after which no further losses should be sustained.

If the clause is construed as a penalty, then it will not be enforceable and the injured party will have to claim for unliquidated damages (assessed by the court).

The obvious advantages of a liquidated damages clause are:

- The fixing of a set amount in advance of any breach, providing both parties with a clearer picture of the financial consequences and thus making it easier to negotiate a price, which will include suitable insurance costs to cover any claims

- The ability of the buyer to deduct any liquidated damages from the payment of the purchase price before sending on the balance (a right of 'set-off'). This avoids the need to go to court and run into the inevitable problems of cost and delay.

These benefits have to be offset against the risks that the buyer's clause may entitle him to less compensation than the actual loss sustained, and the possibility that it may be challenged as a penalty clause.

Liquidated Damages and Penalties

- LD are enforceable; penalties are void
- LD are genuine pre-estimates of losses for breach of contract
- penalties are attempts to coerce performance
- terminology in contract is not conclusive
- excessive amounts = penalty ("unfair, extravagant and unconscionable" – *Dunlop Co Ltd v New Garage Ltd*)
- single sum claimable for all/any type of breach
- should have some maximum limit for compensation
- should not be a compromise figure
- LD fixes claimable sum even if inaccurate

Unliquidated Damages

In the absence of a contractual provision covering damages (or if there is one but it is held to be a penalty clause) it will be necessary to resort to the courts in order to claim compensation for a breach of contract.

Judges attempt to give business effect to the contract – to put the parties in the same financial position they would have been in if the contract had been properly performed.

[Unlike the U.S, punitive damages - acting as a deterrent to future breaches of contract - are not awarded]

Where there is an available market in which the goods can be purchased or sold elsewhere, the difference between the original contract price and the price paid/obtained subsequently will determine available damages (The Market Rule).

e.g.   Seller fails to deliver goods to buyer (original contract price - £12,000) Buyer now has to obtain goods from a different seller and pays £13500. Court will award £1500 to buyer in order to achieve the above objective.

Where there is no such market, loss of profit is the measure of damages.

There is an important restriction on the ability of the injured party to recover for loss suffered from a breach of contract. Claimable loss must have been reasonably foreseeable at the time of the contract as likely to arise from breach of the contract. This is known as the ***Rule in Hadley v Baxendale***. It has the following consequences:

- Natural loss which is the direct consequence of the breach is claimable e.g. predictable costs incurred by the injured party including replacement purchases, loss of normal profits from lost orders dependent on the original goods arriving on time;

- Unusual loss is not claimable unless the other party was informed of it at the time the contract was agreed.

Cases Putting Rule into Practice

Hadley v Baxendale

A mill belonging to Hadley had a broken shaft. It made a contract with a firm of hauliers to take the shaft to a manufacturer for it to be copied and a new one made. The hauliers were in breach of contract by delaying delivery beyond a reasonable length of time. In the meantime, the mill had been at a standstill. A claim for this lost production was brought against the hauliers. **HELD:** The mill was unusual in not possessing a reserve mill shaft. The hauliers had not been informed about this state of affairs and would not have foreseen its occurrence. The claim for lost production was not allowed

Victoria Laundry v Newman Industries

V bought from N a boiler for use in his laundry. Delivery was to be made on 5th June but was not made until November. V claimed:

- loss of the profits the laundry would have made had the boiler been delivered in time;

- loss of profit from some highly profitable dyeing contracts.

  HELD: the laundry profits lost were recoverable, as N must have contemplated their loss if there was delay; the loss on the dyeing contracts, which could not have been contemplated, could not be recovered.

A party may be liable for consequences which, although within the reasonable contemplation of the parties, are significantly more serious than would have been expected:

Parsons (Livestock) Ltd v Uttley Ingham & Co

The claimants, who bred pigs, purchased a food hopper from the defendants. The latter were negligent in their erection of the hopper in that they failed to unseal a ventilator at the top of the hopper. This caused the pig food which was subsequently stored in the hopper to become mouldy. When fed to the pigs they contracted a rare intestinal disease from which they all died.

HELD: The defendants were liable for the loss. It was predictable that food stored in the hopper would become unfit for consumption if not properly ventilated. Once this was established, all the consequent losses were recoverable, even though the seriousness of the illness was not predictable.

What "damage" can be claimed for breach of contract?

- Physical injury resulting
- Damage to property
- Economic loss.

Economic loss includes direct consequential losses such as lost profits and liability for breach of contract to customers resulting from the initial breach.

The Breach must Cause the Damage

Sometimes, although a contract has been broken and damage sustained, it can be argued that the cause of the injury was some other, supervening event. There is a break in the chain of causation between the breach and the damage. The claim would be defeated on this argument.

Lambert v Lewis

A farmer had been held primarily liable for a motoring accident resulting in the death of 2 people. He had been negligent in failing to remedy a defective towing hitch which had resulted in a trailer becoming detached and crashing into a saloon car. He sought to claim damages for breach of contract against the dealer from whom he had bought the hitch (on the grounds of lack of fitness for purpose – there was already a design weakness inherent in the part). **HELD:** The cause of the farmer's loss was his own negligence in failing to repair the hitch when the defect had become known to him. Therefore, the breach by the dealer had not caused his loss. His action failed.

Sometimes the basis of the claim will be limited to lost expenditure, rather than lost revenue. This could be the case where it is virtually impossible to quantify potential revenue losses:

Anglia TV v Reed

The claimants incurred considerable expenditure preparing for a television play. A contract had been agreed with the actor Oliver Reed who was to play the lead role. He broke the contract by refusing to perform the part. Despite making reasonable efforts to find a replacement, no-one was found and the production was cancelled. Anglia claimed for the lost expenditure, partly because of the difficulties of predicting the future success of the play (lost revenue). **HELD:** They were entitled to claim on the basis of wasted expenditure. In other words, **speculative loss** is not recoverable.

Mitigation of Loss

The injured party is under a duty to take reasonable steps to minimise the loss suffered as a consequence of the breach of contract. Thus, replacement goods of a similar specification and quality should be purchased and not more expensive, upmarket ones. The court would not allow such unnecessary expenditure to be compensated for in the award.

Payzu Ltd v Saunders

A contract had been agreed for the sale of fabric, delivery and payment to be made by instalment. When the buyer was late in making the first payment, the supplier refused to make any further deliveries unless they were paid for in cash. The buyer refused to accept this change and sued for breach of contract. **HELD:** The supplier had no right to repudiate the contract for the late payment and was therefore in breach. However, the buyer should have mitigated his losses by accepting the offer of cash on delivery terms. The damages award was restricted to what he would have lost under those terms, namely, interest over the repayment period.

Anticipatory Breach

Sometimes, a party is given advance warning of a future breach of contract. The defaulting party indicates its intention to default e.g. fail to deliver the goods, do the work or pay for the goods/services supplied. In this situation, the injured party is entitled to bring a legal claim as soon as they are informed (*Hochster v De La Tour*). It does not have to wait until the breach actually takes place. This is called anticipatory breach of contract. Of course, the injured party may wish to delay such action in the hope that the other party can be persuaded to carry out its obligations. The only risk in doing so arises if a frustrating event occurs in the meantime. The contract would then become void, disallowing any claim for breach (*Avery v Bowden*)

In Conclusion

- Damages can be either stipulated in the contract (liquidated damages) or assessed by the court (unliquidated damages)

- Liquidated damages clauses (LD's) are a genuine pre-estimate of the likely loss to be suffered from a breach of the contract and are enforceable

- Penalty clauses are punitive attempts to coerce performance and are void

- LD's are binding even if inaccurate – any shortfall cannot then be recovered

- Unliquidated damages attempt to place the injured party in the same position as if the contract had been properly performed

- It is possible to claim for personal injury, damage to property and economic loss caused by a breach of contract

- The rules in Hadley v Baxendale limit damages to those which are reasonably foreseeable at the time of the contract

- The breach must cause the damage

- Speculative losses are not recoverable

- The injured party must mitigate his losses – take reasonable steps to minimise the losses

- An injured party can bring an immediate claim where he is given advance notification of a future breach of contract (anticipatory breach)

Chapter 8
Exclusion Clauses

Clearly it is in the supplier's interests to limit or completely exclude responsibility for damage or loss sustained as a result of breach of contract or negligence on its part. The following chapter examines how the law has changed in recent years and how it is becoming increasingly difficult for suppliers to attach enforceable exclusions to contracts. The chapter concentrates on the following issues:

- Exclusion – definition, justification and dangers
- Common law restrictions – reasonable notification
- Common law restrictions – contra proferentem
- Unfair Contract Terms Act 1977 – main provisions
- Test of reasonableness
- Cases illustrating the test.

Background Issues

An exclusion (or exemption) clause is a term in a contract which seeks to exempt one of the parties from liability in certain events. These include non-performance of contract, defective performance, misrepresentation and negligence.

Between parties of equal bargaining strength such clauses may be legitimate and can serve useful purposes. They can operate as a form of pricing policy by which firms can reduce their prices in exchange for lowering their obligations. It also enables firms to avoid the use of lawyers and the courts, against which they have a traditional distrust.

Problems arise however where there is an inequality of bargaining strength. Potential abuses can be the result of consumer ignorance of their existence in the contract, inability to understand their meaning or inability to resist their inclusion.

The law has a dilemma if it attempts to intervene where abuses are happening. Contract law is built on the doctrine of laissez faire which requires the state to leave the parties alone to make their own arrangements. It is for the parties to make sure that they make a sound deal and must live with the consequences without the "luxury" of being rescued by the courts subsequently.

This harsh position has been modified as the problems of abuse and the growing number of consumer transactions has compelled a change of approach. Initially, the common law introduced a number of restrictions on exclusion clauses (see below) but these were always piece-meal and very limited in operation. Eventually, Parliament passed legislation which provided more significant barriers or restrictions to the use of these clauses. The most important Act in this area is the *Unfair Contract Terms Act 1977*, whose provisions will need to be studied closely. More recently, the European Union has required member countries to satisfy the requirements of the *Unfair Contract Terms Directive*. The UK has issued regulations in 1994 to meet this requirement. These regulations have recently been revised in the light of experience and are now entitled the Unfair Terms in Consumer Contracts Regulations 1999. Clearly these regulations do not apply to contracts made between businesses.

Exclusion Clauses - Common Law Restrictions

The common law established two barriers to the abuse of exemption clauses.

Test 1: Was the Clause a Term of the Contract at all?

There is a general principle of contract which states that no term will be effective and binding unless the other party was given reasonable notice of its existence by the time the contract is completed. Examples of unreasonable notice include:

a) After the contract has already been made.

Olley v Marlborough Court Hotel

A husband and wife booked into an hotel. Their bedroom had a notice limiting liability for lost or stolen articles unless handed to the manageress for safe keeping. Furs belonging to the wife were stolen, partly because of the negligence of the hotel. **HELD** - The notice was ineffective because it was not brought to their attention until after the contract had been made at the reception desk on the ground floor.

b) illegible writing

c) where the exclusion is contained on a piece of paper which the other party is unlikely to consider to be part of the contract :

e.g. on notices which are not obvious to the other party at the time of the contract;

e.g. on a receipt provided as proof of payment. (Whether tickets are contractual documents or mere receipts depends on the circumstances)

Chapelton v Barry UDC

A notice board on promenade stated "Deckchairs for Hire -2d per session of 3 hours. Take one from the stand". When payment was collected later, a ticket was issued which contained an exclusion clause. **HELD** - Unreasonable to communicate conditions by a mere receipt when there was a notice board nearby.

Where the exclusion is contained in the contract and the other party has signed the agreement the general principle is that reasonable notice must be given. It will be no defence to argue that you did not realise what you were signing

L'Estrange v Graucob

A claimant bought a cigarette vending machine and signed a sales agreement which excluded "any express or implied condition, warranty, statutory or otherwise".

HELD - the clause was binding on her even though she had not read the agreement.

Test 2

Did the Exemption Clause Cover the Loss or Damage when Properly Construed?

The courts construe vague or ambigious clauses "contra proferentem" (against the person wishing to rely on the exclusion) so that any ambiguity or doubt will cause it to fail.

Baldry v Marshall

A claimant asked for a car "suitable for touring purposes". The defendant suggested a Bugatti and excluded liability for "any other guarantee, or warranty, statutory or otherwise". **HELD** - the purpose for which the car was required was a condition, not a warranty. The exemption was ineffective.

Andrews v Singer

Andrews agreed to buy some new Singer cars from Singer. Singer excluded "all conditions, warranties and liabilities implied by statute, common law or otherwise". One of the cars supplied was a used car. **HELD** - Exclusion did not cover express terms. Singer were liable for damages.

Various other legal concepts were used by the courts to resist unfair exclusion attempts. These included the doctrine of fundamental breach, the presence of misrepresentation and the collateral contract.

Ultimately it was recognised that a more comprehensive regulation of exclusion clauses was needed. This led to the passing of the Unfair Contract Terms Act 1977. Two of its main provisions are found on the following pages:

THE UNFAIR CONTRACT TERMS ACT 1977

Section 2 (Negligence Liability)

Any attempt to exclude liability for death or personal injury caused by negligence is void (**Section 2(1)**)

Any attempt to exclude liability for damage to property or financial loss caused by negligence is void, unless proved to be fair & reasonable in the circumstances (**Section 2(2)**)

Section 3 (Breach of Contract Liability)

Applies to all contracts involving a consumer and to contracts between businesses where standard form documentation is used

Any attempt to exclude liability for breach of contract is void, unless proved to be fair & reasonable in the circumstances.

Factors Used to Decide Fairness (Schedule 2 of the Act)

- Relative bargaining strength
- Presence of any inducements
- Availability of alternative suppliers
- Obviousness of the exclusion to the other party
- Whether goods were manufactured or adapted to the order of the customer
- Presence of known trade customs or previous dealings

Cases Applying the Reasonableness Test

George Mitchell v Finney Lock Seeds Ltd (1983)

Finney Lock were a firm of seed merchants. They contracted to sell to Mitchell 30 lbs of Dutch winter cabbage seed for £201.60. M. planted 63 acres with the seeds. The resultant crop was worthless, partly because the seed which had been delivered was autumn seed not winter seed and partly because, in any case, the seed was of low quality. M sued for damages of £61,000 for loss of profit. F relied on a standard clause in their conditions of sale which limited their liability to replacing the defective seeds or refunding payment.

HELD: F's limitation clause was unreasonable and therefore F. were liable to compensate M for loss of profits. The main factor which swayed the House of Lords was that F gave evidence that they attempted to negotiate settlements above the price of the seeds in cases where they considered the customer's complaint to be "genuine" and "justified" – a tacit admission that their limitation clause was unreasonable. Two further factors were in favour of M:

1) F had been negligent in that, irrespective of its quality, the variety of seed supplied to M could not be grown commercially in the area where M's farm was situated;

2) Farmers could not be expected to insure against losses of this kind but F could insure against happenings such as occurred in this case without needing to increase their prices significantly1.

Green (RW) v Cade Bros Farm (1978)

The plaintiffs were seed potato merchants. They had had regular dealings with the defendants who were farmers. These dealings had taken place on the standard conditions of the National Association of Seed Potato Merchants. The conditions provided that:

- Notification of rejection, claim or complaint must be made to the seller within three days after the arrival of the seed at its destination; and

- Any claim for compensation would be limited to the amount of the contract price of the potatoes.

One deal was for 20 tons of King Edward potatoes. In fact the potatoes were infected with a virus which could not be detected by inspection at the time of delivery. As a result the seed was planted and it was not until it came up some eight months later that it was found to be useless. The plaintiffs sued for the price of the potatoes and the defendants counter-claimed for damages for loss of profits.

HELD: The defendants' counter claim for damages for breach of s.14 of the Sale of Goods Act was successful: the clause which required the claim or complaint to be made within three days was unreasonable. The plaintiffs had argued that such a clause was necessary because potato seed was a perishable commodity. The judge accepted that the clause might be reasonable in respect of defects which were discoverable upon reasonable examination, but where, as here, the defects were latent, the clause was not reasonable.

However, the clause in their contract with the plaintiff limiting the amount of compensation payable was reasonable, and because of this, damages were limited to the contract price. The factors which influenced the court were:

- The defendants had dealt with the plaintiffs for many years on terms which included the limitation clause;

- The terms had been the subject of discussion between the National Association of Seed Potato Merchants and the National Farmers Union; and

- Although it would have been difficult for the defendants to have obtained seed potatoes from a merchant other than on the condition in the contract with the plaintiffs, it was possible to obtain seed stock certified by the Ministry of Agriculture as being virus free, but at a much higher price.

St Albans City & District Council V International Computers Limited (1995)

The council entered into a contract with ICL for a computer system which it required to determine a new community charge. The software was defective and as a result the charge was set at too low a level. The council brought an action for breach of contract and negligent misrepresentation. ICL relied on their limitation clause which limited its liability to £100,000. The council had objected to this limit during negotiations but did not pursue the issue because of time pressures.

HELD: ICL was fully liable for the loss. The contract had been entered into on the written standard terms of business of ICL within section 3 of UCTA. In deciding that the limitation was unreasonable the following factors were taken into account:

- ICL was a large company in a strong bargaining position and in a better position to bear losses than St Albans, which would have to meet losses out of an increased community charge or reduced services.

- The limitation of £100,000 bore no relation to ICL's insurance cover of £50m.

- St Albans had not been offered any inducement, such as a reduction in price, to accept the limitation and they had no opportunity of getting better terms elsewhere because other suppliers were offering similar terms.

Recent court decisions have shown a growing tendency for judges to expect commercial buyers to be sufficiently sophisticated to look after themselves. Consequently, they are proving less willing to declare exclusion clauses invalid on grounds of unreasonableness.

N.B. Section 3 covers substantially different performance of a contract as well as breach of contract i.e. where, although there is technically no breach of contract, the manner of performance has become significantly different to the one originally proposed. A pre UCTA case which illustrates this situation is:

Anglo Continental Holidays Ltd v Typaldos Lines Ltd

The claimant had booked Mediterranean holiday cruises on behalf of clients with the defendant. Typaldos substituted an older, inferior ship and a less interesting schedule of events less than a fortnight before the scheduled sailing date. The defendant argued it was not in breach of contract, relying on the following exclusion clause:

"Steamers, sailing dates, rates and itineraries are subject to change without prior notice."

HELD: [Pre UCTA], the court decided that such a radical departure from the original contract arrangement could not be covered legitimately by an exclusion. [Post UCTA, the court would rely on the test of reasonableness as the basis for declaring this clause void.]

N.B. Section 6 UCTA regulates attempts by a seller to disclaim responsibility for breaking the implied duties (relating to the goods) found in the Sale of Goods Act 1979. We shall examine its content after we have looked at the implied duties (see Chapter 10)

Exclusion v Insurance

One of the factors used by the courts to decide the reasonableness of an exclusion or limitation clause is the issue of insurance. Selling defective goods or providing substandard services is clearly a risk of business. As such, two alternatives approaches can be taken:

■ Obtain insurance cover and use the policy to pay compensation

■ Use exclusion/limitation clauses in contracts with customers.

The courts will want to establish how costly and difficult it would have been for the supplier to obtain insurance in the circumstances to help decide whether it was appropriate to opt for disclaimers. If it was not expensive or impracticable to obtain insurance, the court may well conclude that its exclusion clause is void through unreasonableness. Hence it is important for organisations to carefully consider the possibilities of insurance when deciding how to protect themselves against breach of contract and negligence liability.

In recent years, the courts have shown an increased reluctance to declare exclusions unreasonable where both parties are commercial undertakings.

In Conclusion

- Exclusion clauses attempt to deny (or limit) liability for such events as breach of contract, negligence and misrepresentation

- Although freedom of contract (laissez faire) restricted legal intervention where abuses occurred, there have always been some curbs on their effectiveness

- Common law restrictions included the requirement of reasonable notification and the contra proferentem rule of interpretation in cases of ambiguity

- The Unfair Contract Terms Act (UCTA) 1977 introduced far more extensive restrictions

- Some exclusions are banned by UCTA e.g. death or injury caused by negligence

- The test of reasonableness has become the basis of regulation in most situations, with a presumption against validity

- A non-exhaustive list of criteria to help decide reasonableness is contained in UCTA

Chapter 9
Frustration of Contract and Force Majeure Clauses

In extreme situations, the courts will allow a party to be excused performance of a contract – where events outside the control of the parties make its performance impossible, illegal or a commercial nonsense. The doctrine of frustration of contract is being applied. It is reluctantly granted, the courts being aware of the possibility of the doctrine being used as a way out of contracts which are no longer desired or profitable. For these reasons parties often include a provision in the contract allowing for suspension or cancellation. These are called force majeure clauses. These can more easily be brought into operation and contain other advantages. The following chapter covers the following legal principles:

- Frustration – definition
- Examples of frustration – physical impossibility, subsequent illegality, basis of contract removed, frustration of commercial purpose
- Effect of doctrine on the contract
- Force majeure clauses – reasons for use and benefits
- Effect on the contract
- Relevance of UCTA 1977

Frustration of Contract

Until the 19th century, the obligation to perform contract was absolute. If it became physically impossible for a party to perform his side of the bargain, he nevertheless had to pay damages for breach, and if external events took away the whole purpose of the contract without the fault of either party, the parties still had to continue with the agreement.

Starting with the case of *Taylor v Caldwell* (1863) the courts have developed the doctrine of frustration of contract. If some event occurs, for which neither party is responsible and which makes total nonsense of the original agreement, then the contract will be discharged by frustration. A radical change in circumstances can sometimes, therefore, be pleaded by a party as a valid excuse for not performing his side of the bargain. This doctrine must be approached with caution, however, because the courts have understandably been reluctant to accept anything but the most fundamental events. The following are the main examples: -

1   Subsequent Physical Impossibility

This will occur where, after the contract was made, it becomes physically impossible or impracticable to perform it. (If it were already impossible when the contract was made, the agreement would be void through fundamental mistake from the outset).

Taylor v Caldwell

A music hall hired for a series of concerts was burnt down before the date for the first performance. This was held to frustrate the contract, because there was no longer any hall to hire. The hirer, therefore, no longer had to pay.

However, a contract will not be frustrated if the goods that have been destroyed can be obtained by the seller from other sources in time for them to be delivered to the buyer.

Robinson v Davison

A pianist, who was engaged to give a concert on a specified, became ill and was incapable of appearing. It was held that this frustrated the contract.

2   Subsequent Illegality

This will occur where, after the contract was made, a change in the law or in the circumstances renders it illegal to perform the agreement.

Avery v Bowden

The contract to load a cargo at Odessa was eventually discharged by the outbreak of the Crimean War, which made it illegal to trade with the enemy.

The imposition of a trade embargo will have the same effect

3   Basis of the Contract Removed

The contract may be frustrated where both parties made it on the basis of a future event that does not take place.

Chandler v Webster

The contract was for the hire of a room in Pall Mall for the day of Edward VII's coronation procession. The rent was over £140, because the procession would pass directly beneath the window. Unfortunately the coronation was postponed when the King became ill. This was held to frustrate the contract. The entire basis of the contract had been removed.

4   Frustration of the Commercial Purpose of the Contract

A change may occur which makes a total nonsense of what was originally agreed, so that what the parties would have to perform bears no relation to what was originally intended. This change must be radical; an event that merely makes it more difficult or expensive for a party to perform the contract will be no excuse. It is rare for a contract to be frustrated on this ground.

Metropolitan Water Board v Dick, Kerr & Co

A firm of contractors agreed in 1914 to build a reservoir. In 1916, under wartime emergency powers, the government requisitioned the plant for the war effort. This was held to frustrate the contract. Although it might eventually be possible to start work again after the war, the enforced hold-up for an indefinite period made nonsense of the contract.

c.f. Davis Contractors v Fareham UDC

Builders contracted with Fareham Council to build 78 houses for a fixed sum within a period of eight months. Owing to lack of adequate supplies of labour it took the builders 22 months to complete the work. The costs of building having risen, the builders claimed that their contract with the council was frustrated and that they were entitled to a higher sum than the contract price (based on a claim for quantum meruit – as much as is deserved). **HELD**: What had taken place was an unexpected turn of events that made the contract more onerous than had been contemplated, but this did not operate to frustrate the contract.

If a seller wishes to protect himself against liability to the buyer for delays due to such matters as strikes or non-delivery of raw materials, he should make special provision for this in the contract (See Force Majeure Clauses below)

Frustrated Contracts – Consequences

Frustration automatically brings the contract to an end and renders it void. As a general rule, all sums paid by either party in pursuance of the contract before it was discharged are recoverable, and all sums not yet paid cease to be due. However, the *Law Reform (Frustrated Contracts) Act 1943* modifies this in the following way:

If one party has, before the time of discharge, incurred expenses in performing it, the court may in its discretion, allow him to keep or recover all or part of sums already paid or due under the contract.

Force Majeure Clauses

The doctrine of frustration of contract is sometimes available to sellers who find that performance of the contract has become either impossible or a commercial nonsense. The doctrine operates where intervening events have taken place which are outside their control. There are however serious risks in relying on the doctrine if problems in performance arise. The courts interpret the doctrine narrowly and strictly and they frequently refuse to accept its use.

It is often considered wiser to introduce into contracts a clause defining in advance the rights and duties of the parties if certain events beyond their control occur, whether or not such events would result, in legal terms, in frustration of the contract. Such a clause is known as a force majeure clause.

Force majeure events are events which are beyond the control of the parties and the expression has been judicially defined in one case to cover "all circumstances beyond the will of man, and which it is not in his power to control, and such force majeure is sufficient to justify the non-execution of a contract." Thus, war, fire, flood, other natural disasters and epidemics can constitute force majeure events as well as the strikes of workmen. However, it is important to realise that, in English law, there is no official definition of the concept and it will be a matter for each individual contract to provide its own definition of what represents force majeure. Sellers' terms and conditions will often include an extensive list of events. Buyers' terms will be narrower and often specifically exclude events such as unofficial strike action.

The effect of the force majeure event is to bring the clause into operation and, in accordance with its terms, the contract is either suspended or discharged by agreement. This prevents claims for breach of contract being brought by the other party.

Although the wording of these clauses varies according to the nature of the contract, most sale of goods agreements contain wording similar to the following:

Strikes, lockouts, labour disturbances, anomalous working conditions, accident to machinery, delays en route, policies or restrictions of governments, including restrictions of export and other licences, or any other contingency whatsoever beyond seller's control, including war, to be sufficient excuse for any delay or non-fulfilment traceable to any of these causes.

In other words, a list of possible force majeure events capable of impeding or preventing performance are provided, together with a 'sweeping-up' phrase designed to ensure that there are no gaps in the formula.

The clause will then provide for the parties to suspend or cancel the contract depending on the circumstances. The parties are usually under a duty to keep each other notified regarding their respective positions.

Benefits of Force Majeure Clauses

- Wider range of events can be included to escape performance than is possible using the doctrine of frustration

- No need to resort to litigation as would be likely if frustration of contract was being argued

- More flexible options are possible – suspension of the contract instead of contract always becoming void under the doctrine of frustration

Force majeure clauses are a variety of exclusion clause and therefore subject to the legal restrictions imposed on such clauses. The most important control is found in section 3 of the Unfair Contract Terms Act 1977 and subjects the clause to the test of reasonableness in the circumstances. As a general rule, most standard force majeure clauses are seen to satisfy this test, the event or events causing the delay or non-performance being outside the control of the seller.

In Conclusion

- The doctrine of frustration of contract excuses performance where subsequent events outside the parties control render it impossible, illegal or a commercial nonsense to expect performance to take place

- The doctrine is strictly and narrowly interpreted and operates in only a small number of extreme situations

- These exceptions are subsequent physical impossibility, subsequent illegality, basis of contract removed and frustration of the commercial purpose of the contract

- Frustrated contracts become void and a number of rules aimed at restoring the original position are set out in the *Law Reform (Frustrated Contracts) Act 1943*

- Force majeure clauses strengthen the position of the supplier (and occasionally the buyer) in providing a longer list of events entitling suspension and/or cancellation of the contract

- Force majeure clauses are a variety of exclusion and therefore subject to the test of reasonableness set out in *UCTA 1977 (section 3).*

Chapter 10
Statutory Protection - Buyer's Rights

2 Sale of Goods - Supply of Services

Contracts have been increasingly regulated by legislation during the C20 especially in the context of consumer agreements. We now need to examine the rights which have been extended to buyers (commercial as well as consumer) through the incorporation of implied terms into sale of goods contracts and contracts for services (whether for work and materials or for pure services).

The chapter covers the following legal principles and issues:

- Background to Sale of Goods Act 1979 (SOGA) – a laissez faire Act
- Implied duties of a seller under SOGA
- Cases illustrating infringements of implied duties
- Changes introduced in 1994
- Exclusion of implied terms
- Specific rules relating to delivery to delivery of wrong quantity
- Instalment deliveries and defective performance
- Implied duties of a supplier in contracts for services under Supply of Goods and Services Act 1982.

Sale of Goods Acts

Traditionally the most important type of contract (in terms of volume and value) is sale of goods. The law regulating sale of goods is predominantly statutory with the Sale of Goods Act 1979 forming its core. The 1979 Act has been amended several times to reflect changing commercial practice, most significantly in 1994. This Act is an example of laissez faire legislation, which (apart from a few exceptions) does not impose its provisions on the parties to the contract. They are left free to draft their rights and duties and depart from those specified in the Act. The Act can be seen as a "fall-back" code of principles, which applies where the parties have not agreed their position. That is why many of the sections in the Act begin with the expression "Unless otherwise agreed...".

Some of its most important provisions from the point of view of buyers' rights are found in ss. 12-15. These provide a series of obligations imposed on the seller relating to his rights to sell, and the description, quality and fitness of the goods in question. The ability of the seller to exclude liability for infringing these implied duties has been severely constrained since the passing of the Unfair Contract Terms Act 1979, in particular, section 6 (see later). As such they represent something of an exception to the liberal, laissez faire approach indicated above. The following page contains the main provisions:

SALE OF GOODS ACT 1979

SECTION 12

THE SELLER MUST HAVE THE RIGHT TO SELL (GOOD TITLE)

SECTION 13

WHERE THERE IS A CONTRACT TO SELL GOODS BY DESCRIPTION, THE GOODS MUST CORRESPOND WITH THE DESCRIPTION

SECTION 14(2)

WHERE THE SELLER SELLS GOODS IN THE COURSE OF A BUSINESS, THE GOODS MUST BE OF SATISFACTORY QUALITY

Goods will be of satisfactory quality if they meet the standard that a reasonable person would regard as satisfactory, taking account of any description of the goods, the price if relevant, and all other relevant circumstances.

The quality of goods includes their state and condition, which can include the following: -

a) fitness for all the purposes for which goods of the kind in question are commonly supplied;

b) appearance and finish;

c) freedom from minor defects;

d) safety; and

e) durability

SECTION 14(3)

WHERE THE SELLER SELLS IN THE COURSE OF A BUSINESS AND THE BUYER MAKES KNOWN TO THE SELLER ANY PARTICULAR PURPOSE FOR WHICH THE GOODS ARE BEING BOUGHT, THE GOODS SUPPLIED MUST BE REASONABLY FIT FOR THAT PURPOSE

SECTION 15

WHERE GOODS ARE SOLD BY SAMPLE, THE BULK MUST CORRESPOND

Breach of Contract – Strict Liability

It is important to realise that breach of contract is based on the concept of strict liability. In other words, the injured party does not have to prove that the defendant was to blame or was at fault in order to succeed. It is regarded as a risk of business that firms who break contracts are liable even if they are not to blame for the failure. However, where a firm has been made liable for supplying faulty goods, they in turn can bring a claim against their suppliers for breach of contract

The Implied Conditions – Detail and Cases

Section 12 (Title)

This has been described as the most important obligation of all those imposed on the seller. The entire basis of the contract (and the consideration for the price) is the passing on of ownership to the buyer.

Rowland v Divall

The claimant dealer bought a car from the defendant in May. He sold it in July, but in September the police took possession of the vehicle on the ground that it was a stolen car and that the person who had sold it to the defendant had no title to sell it. The claimant sued to recover the price that he had paid the defendant for the car.

HELD: He was entitled to succeed as the defendant had been in breach of Section 12

There are two implied warranties also found in Section 12 relating to the buyer receiving goods without encumbrances and having quiet possession of the goods. This covers such issues as goods being subject to patents and liens.

Section 13 (Description)

"Description" applies to such matters as specification of goods, weight, ingredients and composition. The description has to be in the contract itself, although previous adverts have been held to be relevant in descriptions of the goods.

The rule is a strict one and minor discrepancies have given buyers the right to cancel the contract.

Arcos Ltd v Ronaasen & Son

Suppliers agreed to deliver half inch wooden staves for use in building work (there was no margin of tolerance indicated in the agreement). When they arrived, the purchaser claimed to reject them on the ground that they did not correspond with the description in that some were slightly above and some were slightly below the required width.

HELD: They were entitled to reject (even though all would have been usable by the purchaser without any disadvantage).

Re Moore & Landauer

A contract was agreed for the sale of canned fruit to be packed in cases, each case to contain 30 tins. On delivery about half of the cases contained 24 tins. The total delivered was however correct.

HELD: The buyer was able to reject the entire consignment (again, even though no commercial disadvantage had been sustained by the purchaser)

More recently a less rigorous approach has been evident where minor infringements have been seen as entitling the buyer only to claim damages (as if a warranty had been broken instead). Since 1994, Section 15(A) of the Act now requires trade buyers to treat minor breaches of any of the implied conditions as breach of warranties. The standard is what a reasonable person would judge to be minor. Consumers can still reject for minor infringements.

The section only applies if the sale involved is "by description". This applies to almost all sales e.g. all orders for unascertained or future goods, and even sales of identified goods selected by customers in shops. Possible the only situation where it does not apply is where the seller shows the buyer the goods in question and immediately states that they are to be sold "just as they are, with no guarantees attached". This may then disconnect the goods from any "description" that would otherwise attach to them.

The buyer must have relied on the description before the section applies.

Harlingdon & Leinster Enterprises Ltd V Christopher Hull Fine Art Ltd

The defendant art dealer had been asked to sell two paintings which had been described in an auction catalogue as being painted by Gabrielle Munter, an important German Expressionist. The dealer was not an expert in this school of painting. He contacted the plaintiffs who were specialists in this field. Having looked at the painting they decided to buy one of the paintings for £6000. This decision was taken despite the defendant having made clear that he did not know much about the paintings and that he was not an expert in that field. The painting was in fact a forgery and the plaintiff claimed breach of Section 13 to obtain repayment of the purchase price.

HELD: Their action must fail. There had not been a sale by description. The buyers were basing their decision on their own inspection of the painting and not on any statements as to origin by the dealer.

Section 14 (2)   (Satisfactory Quality)

The sale must be in the course of a business. This is not limited to dealers in the goods in question but extends to any organisation which finds itself selling some goods in the course of its operations e.g. car rental firm selling its existing stock to buy new; professional firms selling office equipment to buy new. Public sector organisations such as local councils can therefore also sell in the course of a business in this situation.

What is "satisfactory quality"? The standard is what a reasonable person would regard as satisfactory in the circumstances. [Section 14(2)(A)] This should take into account such issues as the price paid, whether the goods are new or second hand, and any description applied to them. The new consumer focus has introduced new criteria in deciding what is satisfactory - fitness for purpose (a previous one); appearance, freedom from minor defects, safety and durability [Section 14(2) (B)].

The section does not apply to defects which have been specifically brought to the buyer's attention before the contract is concluded.

It also does not apply to obvious defects which should have been detected by the buyer if he has had the opportunity to examine the goods prior to sale.

Wilson v Rickett, Cockerell & Co

The claimant and her husband sued the defendant coal merchants for damage to their dining room caused by an explosion in the firegrate. This was caused by a detonator having been admixed in the coalite purchased.
HELD: This was a breach of satisfactory quality.

The standard need not be significantly demanding, particularly in the context of second hand goods, and to a smaller extent, commercial (as against consumer) contracts.

Cehave NV v Bremer Handelsgesellschaft mbH (The Hansa Nord Case)

A cargo of citrus pulp pellets which had been damaged through overheating whilst in transit was held to be of "merchantable quality" (the pre 1994 equivalent of satisfactory quality). The court accepted that the goods were far from perfect. However, they had remained saleable for the purpose for which they could normally be bought. The pellets were bought to be fed to cattle and were still capable of fulfilling this purpose. It would seem the Court took the view that the reasonable commercial buyer would have considered obtaining a discount as a more appropriate approach rather than rejecting the consignment.

Section 14 (3)   (Fitness for Purpose)

As with the previous condition, this only applies if the sale is in the course of a business. In addition it will only apply if the buyer has made known to the seller the particular purpose for which the goods are to be used. This can be done expressly (through discussion etc.) or by implication (where the goods have only one normal use - food, clothing, cars, washing machines etc.). It becomes important to inform the seller of special uses and seek reliance on his judgement where the goods can be used in a range of situations. (e.g. needing a car which will be capable of being used on a hill farm in muddy conditions).

Frost v Aylesbury Dairy Co

The defendant milk dealers supplied the claimant with milk for himself and his family. On one occasion, the milk contained typhoid bacteria from which his wife contracted typhoid and died. The husband brought a claim for breach of Section 14(3).

HELD: The claim was successful. It was irrelevant that the defendants had not been negligent. Breach of contract is based on strict liability.

Section 15 (Sample)

This is less extensive in application. It only applies when it is customary for a sample to be shown prior to a contract being agreed. Examples in consumer sales include contracts for the sale of carpets, furnishings (curtains etc.) and in some situations, sale of paint. In the trade context, sale of bulk chemicals will often be preceded by a sample.

Compliance with the sample is strict. However, remember that since 1994, trade buyers may have to treat minor infringements as a breach of warranty only, depriving them of any right to refuse delivery and cancel the contract.

Sale and Supply of Goods Act 1994

This Act made significant modifications to the 1979 Act, the main examples of which are outlined below. It is important to understand that the 1994 Act did not in any way 'replace' the earlier one. It simply altered its provisions so that new copies of the 1979 Act contain amended sections. It is still the 1979 Act that forms the basis of sale of goods law in the UK.

Replacement of "Merchantable Quality"

One of the recommendations of the Law Commission was that there should be changes to section 14(2) of the *Sale of Goods Act 1979* (SOGA) which stated that where the seller sells goods in the course of a business there is an implied term that the goods supplied shall be of merchantable quality. This has now been replaced by an expanded text which sets a rather higher standard by the substitution of the phrase "satisfactory quality".

The new Act prescribes that the quality of goods shall include their state and condition and the following other matters where appropriate:-

a) Fitness for all the purposes for which goods of the kind in question are commonly supplied

b) Appearance and finish

c) Freedom from minor defects

d) Safety

e) Durability.

The 1994 Act also makes some minor amendments as compared with the former definition of merchantable quality. It prescribes that goods are of satisfactory quality if they meet the standard that a reasonable person would regard as satisfactory, taking account of any description of the goods, the price if relevant and all other relevant circumstances. It retains the present exclusions in respect of matters making the quality of goods unsatisfactory which are drawn to the buyer's attention before the contract is made or which ought to have been revealed by a buyer's examination of the goods or a sample of them.

Virtually the same definition of "satisfactory quality" is imported into the implied terms where goods are supplied on hire or hire purchase or the other circumstances mentioned earlier.

Acceptance and Rejection

Another area of the law that has given rise to problems is the question whether a buyer of goods which turn out to be unsatisfactory has a right to reject them. The Act makes two main changes here.

Where goods are delivered to the buyer and he has not previously examined them, he will in future not be deemed to have accepted them until he has a reasonable opportunity of examining them to ascertain whether they are in conformity with the contract and, where appropriate, with any sample. Furthermore, where the buyer deals as consumer, he will not lose his right to examine the goods by agreement, waiver or otherwise.

The Sale of Goods Act 1979 provides that the buyer is deemed to have accepted goods when after the lapse of reasonable time he retains the goods without intimating that he has rejected them. This provision is retained but in addition the buyer is not deemed to have accepted the goods merely because he asks for or agrees to their repair by or under an arrangement with the seller or he delivers the goods to another under a sub-sale. In part this reflects case law since 1979.

Right of Partial Rejection

The Act inserts a new section in the SOGA 1979 (but not in the other Acts modified) giving the buyer a right to reject some of the goods where these are defective and accept the rest.

Trivial Breaches - Commercial Buyer

The Act provides that where a buyer would have the right to reject goods because of a breach of the implied terms as to description, quality or fitness but the breach is so slight that it would be unreasonable for the buyer to reject the goods, then if the buyer does not "deal as consumer" the breach shall not be treated as a breach of condition (giving a right to reject) but may be treated as a breach of warranty (giving rise to a claim for damages). A similar provision applies to hire purchase.

A further clause provides that where a seller delivers a quantity of goods either slightly larger of slightly less than the quantity contracted for, a commercial buyer shall not have the right to reject the whole quantity although he could reject any minor excess. There are no similar clauses in respect of hire purchase, hire or other supplies of goods.

Exclusion of Implied Conditions

Can the seller deny liability for breaking any of the obligations contained in sections 12-15? The *Unfair Contract Terms Act 1977* deals with this issue in section 6:

Section 6 (Liability for breach of ss 12-15 Sale of Goods Act 1979)

S. 12	(Title)	Can never be excluded (void)
Ss 13-15	(Description	
	Satisfactory Quality	Depends type of sale
	Fitness for Purpose	
	Sample)	

Consumer Sales

Where the seller is selling goods in the course of a business (and the goods are of a type normally sold in this situation) and the buyer is purchasing the goods for personal and private use

None of the above implied conditions can be excluded in consumer sales (void)

Non-Consumer Sales

Basically contracts made between two businesses. Both seller and buyer are making the contract in the course of their businesses

Ss. 13 - 15 cannot be excluded by the seller unless proved to be fair and reasonable in the circumstances

[See earlier factors for deciding fairness and reasonableness]

Notices in shops suggesting that customers have no rights to complain constitute a criminal offence apart from being void

e.g.   "No refunds or exchanges allowed"

Sale of Goods – Delivery of Wrong Quantity

Where the wrong quantity is delivered, there is a breach of Section 13 SOGA 1979 – there is a discrepancy between the description of the goods (which includes the quantity involved) and the actual goods supplied. The rights of the buyer are then found in s.30 as amended. The following rules apply:

- If less than contract quantity – buyer can reject or accept and pay at contract rate

- If more than contract quantity – buyer can accept the whole (and pay for surplus at contract rate) or reject the surplus and accept the proper quantity

- If in addition to contract goods, goods of a different description are delivered – buyer can reject all the consignment or just the non contract ones.

- The buyer cannot accept goods of a type not contracted for except under a new contract

Instalment Deliveries and Defective Performance

Whilst on the theme of delivery and breach it may be useful to consider the position of instalment deliveries. Where a contract consists of a series of instalment deliveries the question can arise whether the buyer can terminate the remainder of the contract when a breach of contract has occurred e.g. sub-standard goods have been delivered, or non-delivery of a consignment. In the case of substandard goods or goods which are not of correct specification it is clearly within the rights of the buyer to reject that particular delivery. But can he cancel the remaining deliveries? According to tests laid down in the Maple Flock case (see below), two questions are central to this issue:

- How serious is the breach in comparison to the contract as a whole?
- How likely is it that the breach is likely to be repeated in the future?

Munro & Co v Meyer

The first half of a series of instalments were discovered to be of substandard quality. **Held**: The buyer was entitled to repudiate the contract.

Maple Flock Ltd v Universal Furniture Products Ltd

A single instalment (the sixteenth out of a total of 75) consisted of substandard goods. The buyer repudiated the contract. HELD: Breach of contract by the buyer. (A buyer cannot be compelled to take delivery by instalments unless this was agreed in the contract).

Contracts for Services

These contracts are governed by the *Supply of Goods and Services Act 1982*. Contracts for services are assuming an increasingly important role within the UK economy. Just one reason for this expansion (among many) is the growth of outsourcing. Some services contracts will be for work and materials eg. construction work; others will be purely for services eg. architects, surveyors.

Part 1 of the *Supply of Goods and Services Act* relates to "contracts for the transfer of property in goods" i.e. contracts for work and materials. The supply of goods is governed by Part 1 of the 1982 Act and the services supplied (or the work element) are governed by Part II of the Act.

Contracts of exchange or barter, hire, rental or leasing are governed by Part 1, while contracts for services only, are governed by Part II.

In Part 1 of the Act, Sections 2-5 provide for statutory implied terms on the part of the seller similar to those in S.12-15 of the *Sale of Goods Act 1979*. In other words:

- The supplier must have the right to sell   s.2
- The goods must correspond with description   s.3
- The goods must be of satisfactory quality   s.4(1)
- The goods must be fit for the purpose intended   s.4(2)
- The goods must correspond with sample   s.5

The Supply of Goods and Services Act 1982 includes a number of implied terms relating specifically to services.

Section 13

There is an implied term that where the supplier is acting in the course of a business, the service will be carried out with reasonable care and skill. This requires the contractor to perform the work to a level that is the average, normal level for the type of contractor involved – the market norm if you like. The expected level of skill will therefore vary depending on the type of contractor involved. Mistakes can be made without necessarily infringing this implied duty, provided they are of a sort that would be made by most competent contractors engaged in the work involved. However, when the seriousness of the defective performance is of a higher order, or the frequency of mistakes is greater than the norm, we could well be looking at a breach of s.13. Evidence of the industry norm would need to be provided to the court to support the claim or defence in the case.

Section 14

There is an implied term that where the supplier is acting in the course of a business and the time for the service to be carried out is not fixed by the contract or determined by the course of dealings between the parties, the supplier shall carry out the contract within a reasonable time.

Usually, the contract will have dealt with time for performance (delivery, payment etc). If time has been made of the essence, it is treated as a condition of the contract and entitles the injured party to cancel the contract e.g. for late delivery. Where it has not been made clear, it will depend on the individual circumstances whether it will be a condition, although the courts will often find that it is so. There is a presumption that time for payment is not a condition though.

It is possible to make time for delivery of the essence even where it was not made explicit at the time when the contract was first agreed. This is done by giving notice to the supplier that time is now to be regarded as of the essence. Subject to the period of time for delivery being reasonable, it will now be treated as a condition of the contract:

Rickards (Charles) v Oppenheim

C agreed to sell to O a Rolls Royce chassis with a body built on it, delivery to be made by March 20. It was not delivered then. O pressed for delivery and finally said in June that he would not accept delivery after July 25. Delivery was not made then and O bought another car. Delivery was offered in October but O refused it. C sued for the price. **HELD**, the action failed. O had waived the original time for delivery but was entitled, on giving reasonable notice, to make time of the essence of the contract.

Section 15

There is an implied term that where the consideration is not determined by a contract or by the course of dealings between the parties, the party contracting with the supplier shall pay a reasonable price.

There is a general presumption that estimates are not legally binding whereas quotations are legally binding. However, the court would always look at the individual circumstances of each case and not rely on the heading used.

In Conclusion

- Two Acts imply terms into contracts for sale of goods and provision of services – the Sale of Goods Act (SOGA) 1979 and the Supply of Goods & Services Act (SGSA) 1982

- SOGA 1979 is an example of laissez faire legislation – most of its 'rules' can be modified by contractual provision ("unless otherwise agreed")

- SOGA 1979 creates 5 important implied duties on the seller relating to the goods – the right to sell (title), correspondence with description, satisfactory quality, fitness for purpose and correspondence with sample

- SOGA 1979 has been amended on several occasions (especially in 1994)

- Exclusion of the implied duties is impossible in consumer sales, but still possible in non-consumer sales where it is subject to the test of reasonableness as set out in UCTA 1977 (title can never be excluded though)

- SGSA 1982 (Part One) contains a similar set of implied duties relating to materials supplied under a contract for work and materials or hire; Part Two contains a number of implied duties relating to competency, time and price

- Delivery of the wrong quantity is a breach of section 13 SOGA 1979 (description) and subject to various rights made available to the buyer in section 30

- The ability of the injured party to terminate the rest of an instalment delivery contract for breach of a single instalment (or several) depends on the relative seriousness of the breach compared with the entire contract and the likelihood of repetition

Chapter 11
Transfer of Property

The Sale of Goods Act 1979 uses the expression 'property' to denote ownership of the goods – the seller "agreeing to transfer the property in goods to the buyer in return for a money consideration called the price." The concept of ownership is expressed as 'title' in other parts of the Act. 'Title' tends to be used more when the central issue is the validity of ownership – whether good title or defective title has passed to the buyer.

The SOGA 1979 provides a set of rules relating to when ownership passes from seller to buyer. Once again, the laissez faire approach of the Act is evident by allowing the parties to make their own arrangements, the statutory rules being a fall-back position if it is not possible to establish the parties' intentions.

The chapter covers the following principles and rules:

- Reasons why important to know when property passes from seller to buyer
- Classification of goods – specific and unascertained
- Rules deciding when property passes
- Cases illustrating rules in operation.

The essence of a sale of goods is the passing of ownership from the seller to the buyer. It is important to know not only whether ownership ('property') has transferred but also when it has passed for a number of reasons:

1) It affects the question of risk (who bears the loss for accidents?)

Under s.20 (1) SGA 1979, risk passes with ownership (unless otherwise agreed). This has important implications for insurance purposes. Both parties will wish to minimise the costs of insurance policies and will therefore only insure for the time they are at risk i.e. hold ownership of the goods. This transition of ownership and risk at the same time can be modified by agreement however ('Unless otherwise agreed') e.g. by having a retention of title clause delaying transfer of ownership until payment has been made. The seller will often insist that risk passes upon delivery.

N.B. The party in possession is liable for damage caused by his own negligence – even if ownership belongs to the other party. The goods are being held in a bailee capacity, and as bailee, a duty to take reasonable care of the goods exists.

2) It affects the rights of the liquidator in insolvency proceedings – he cannot sell goods which are not owned by the insolvent company.

When Does Ownership Transfer?

This depends on which category of goods is involved. Are they specific, ascertained goods or unascertained goods?

■ Specific Goods

Goods which have been identified and agreed upon at the time of the sale Examples include buying second-hand vehicles and purchasing food, clothes etc in high street shops and supermarkets.

■ Unascertained Goods

Goods described but not yet identified at the time of sale. Examples include ordering goods by invoice (quantity and specification indicated), purchase of new vehicles and ordering goods by mail order.

Relevant Sections

S.16 states that property in unascertained goods cannot pass until goods of the correct description are ascertained (see s.18 rule 5 below)

S.17 states that property in specific, ascertained goods passes according to the intentions of the parties – judged by the wording of the contract and the circumstances of the case.

The contract may remain silent on the matter though. Then a series of rules found in s.18 decide the outcome.

Section 18

Rule 1 (Specific, ascertained goods in a deliverable state)

In an unconditional contract for the sale of specific goods, in a deliverable state, property passes when the contract is made (even if the time for payment and/or delivery is postponed).

The goods must be 'in a deliverable state'. This is defined in s.62 as "when they are in such a state that the buyer would under the contract be bound to take delivery of them."

Rule 2 (Specific, ascertained goods not in a deliverable state)

If the seller is bound to do something to put the specific goods into a deliverable state, property passes when the action is taken and the buyer notified.

Rule 3 (specific, ascertained goods in a deliverable state but which need to be weighed, measured or tested by the seller to establish the price)

Property will pass when the seller has weighed, measured etc. the goods and notified the buyer.

Rule 4 (specific, ascertained goods sent on approval or sale or return)

Here, property passes: -

- when the buyer approves the transaction either by telling the seller, or doing any other act which adopts the transaction, or,
- when the buyer, without giving notice of rejection, retains the goods for the agreed time, or if no time has been agreed, for a reasonable time.

Rule 5 (unascertained or future goods)

In a contract for the sale of unascertained or future goods identifiable by description, property passes when goods of the correct description in a deliverable state are unconditionally appropriated to the contract by one party with the consent of the other party. Such consent may be express or implied, and may be given either before or after the appropriation is made. On a self-service garage forecourt petrol is pumped by the customer (the buyer) with the consent of the seller. Where the forecourt is attended the seller will make the unconditional appropriation with the consent of the buyer.

The goods must be unconditionally appropriated to the contract. This means irrevocably attached to that contract so that they cannot be use for any other transaction.

Federspiel (Carlos) v Charles Twigg & Co

F., a Costa Rican company, bought from T., an English company, 85 bicycles under a contract providing that T. should ship them in June. F. paid the purchase price in advance. In July a receiver was appointed for T. and all the assets, including the bicycles, were to be sold in the liquidation. F. alleged that as the bicycles had been duly packed into cases, marked with their name, were registered for consignment, and shipping space was reserved for them in a named ship, this setting aside of the goods amounted to an unconditional appropriation and that property had therefore passed to them.

HELD: The intention of the parties was that the property should pass on shipment. There had not yet been an unconditional appropriation. The bicycles could still be unpacked and used in other contracts.

The unconditional appropriation normally takes place on delivery. It could take place earlier though e.g. if the goods have been handed over to an independent carrier without reserving the right of disposal.

The goods must already be in a deliverable state:

Phillip Head and Sons v Showfronts

A buyer ordered carpeting which was to be laid by the house furnishers selling it. The carpets were delivered but were stolen before they could be laid.

HELD: The house furnishers must bear the loss because property had not passed to the buyer. The carpeting was not in a 'deliverable state' until it had been laid and so goods in a deliverable state had not been unconditionally appropriated to the contract.

Retention of Title Clauses (RoT)

During periods when market conditions are difficult and insolvencies more common place, contractors will seek to put themselves in a stronger position than they might otherwise enjoy in reliance upon the Sale of Goods Act 1979. The most common method of achieving this stronger protection is through the use of clauses which allow the contractor to deliver goods but which seek to delay the passing of ownership from the date of delivery to the date upon which payment for the goods is received by the contractor. Some will go further, reserving title not only until the specific goods have been paid for, but until goods delivered under other contracts have also been paid for. Essentially, such clauses are referred to as "reservation of title" clauses or "Romalpa" clauses after the original case in which they were considered in the UK.

The main advantage of retaining ownership is to create greater security in the event of a purchaser going insolvent between receipt of the goods but prior to paying for them.

Although a RoT clause can, in some circumstances, significantly assist a supplier, the degree of protection they afford is frequently misunderstood, with unfortunate consequences for the supplier.

The advantage of an RoT clause is best illustrated by the important decision in:

Aluminium Industrie Vaassen BV v Romalpa Aluminium Ltd ("Romalpa")

AIV sold aluminium to Romalpa, the conditions of sale containing a RoT clause, reserving title until the aluminium had been paid for. Romalpa sold the aluminium but, before it could pay AIV, a Receiver was appointed. AIV claimed that as the aluminium belonged to them and as the proceeds of the sale from the aluminium were identifiable, they could trace their interest into the proceeds of sale and were entitled to these proceeds.

The Court of Appeal upheld AIV's claim.

It was largely as a result of this case and the resulting publicity it received that the use of RoT clauses increased dramatically, as suppliers saw them as a panacea to deal with the problems otherwise caused by the purchaser's insolvency. However, RoT clauses have been considered on a number of occasions by the courts and the protection they afford is not necessarily as broad as might at first appear to be the case.

Firstly, the goods which are the subject of the RoT clause must be tangible. The clause will no longer bite if the goods have ceased to exist as a separate and distinct item. A good example is the case of:

Borden (UK) Ltd v Scottish Timber Products Ltd

Scottish Timber supplied resin which was used by Borden to manufacture chipboard, which was then sold. The resin was supplied on a RoT clause and Borden went into liquidation before Scottish Timber had been paid for the resin. Scottish Timber claimed that their interest in the resin could be traced into the chipboard and then into the proceeds of sale of the chipboard.

The Court of Appeal held that Scottish Timber were not entitled to trace their interest into the proceeds of sale. The resin ceased to have any separated identity once incorporated into the chipboard and the reservation of title clause could not be effective.

Similarly, if the goods are of the 'stand alone' type, a RoT clause may not be fully effective if quantities of goods have been supplied, some of which have been paid for, whilst others have not, and the supplier is unable to demonstrate which particular ones are subject to the RoT clause e.g. by reference to batch numbers, serial numbers or the like on invoices and which have not been paid for.

How effective can RoT clauses be in recovering the proceeds of sale of the goods in question? Where such clauses are used, a Liquidator or Receiver will seek to argue that the RoT clause operates as a floating charge over the assets of the purchaser and is therefore void unless it is registered at Companies House in accordance with the requirements of s. 396 of the Companies Act 1985. This section requires mortgages, floating charges and charges on any goods or of any interest in the goods to be registered.

If the RoT clause seeks to give the supplier an entitlement in the proceeds of the sale of the goods, the clause may be void through lack of registration, unless it succeeds in creating a legal right to trace the interest in the goods into the proceeds of sale.

To achieve this, it would be necessary to require the purchaser to hold the goods in a fiduciary capacity, the proceeds of sale would need to be kept in a distinct and separate account and there might need to be an entitlement to payment on delivery, with the supplier having a discretion not to enforce payment.

RoT clauses should be seen as an addition to well defined payment terms supported by strong credit control measures and appropriate action to recover outstanding monies where necessary.

In Conclusion

- Transfer of property means transfer of ownership.
- It is important to know when ownership passes for reasons of risk (who bears the loss of accidental damage?) and liquidator's rights in the event of insolvency
- It is necessary to know which category of goods is involved to establish the relevant rules governing transfer of ownership – are they specific goods or unascertained goods?
- Specific goods are ones which have been identified and agreed upon at the time of contract –it is known precisely which goods are to be used for that contract; unascertained goods are described (specification, quantity etc.) but not yet identified
- If the contract is silent on the matter, property in specific goods passes according to Rules 1- 4 in section 18 SOGA 1979
- Property in unascertained goods passes according to section 18 Rule 5.

Chapter 12
Transfer of Title

The SOGA 1979 provides a set of rules governing situations where the seller did not have the right to sell the goods. Normally the original owner is protected by the so-called Nemo Dat Doctrine which basically states that you cannot pass on a better title than the one you possess yourself. However, in order to encourage commerce, the Act has created a number of exceptions where protection is given to the innocent buyer who will be able to keep the goods and resist claims for repossession by the original owner. The chapter covers:

- The basic position – nemo dat doctrine
- Exceptions
- Cases illustrating exceptions.

Problems may arise where the seller did not have the right to sell the goods that have been purchased in good faith by an innocent buyer. Examples include stolen goods, goods obtained by deception and goods in the possession of someone who has no authority to sell. One of two innocent parties will have to lose out – either the original owner or the innocent third party purchaser.

The general rule is that property rights will be protected and therefore the original owner will be able to recover the goods from the third party purchaser. The doctrine known as 'Nemo Dat Quod Non Habet' is applied ('No-one can give a better title than the one they themselves possess'). This is stated in s.21 (1) SGA 1979. All that the buyer can do here is to bring an action for breach of contract against the seller (breach of s.12 Sale of Goods Act 1979 – seller must have the right to sell). However, this doctrine has been the subject of a large number of exceptions intended to protect buyers and encourage commerce. The following are the most important examples:

- Estoppel
- Sale by a mercantile agent
- Sale under a voidable title
- Sale by a seller in possession
- Sale by a buyer in possession
- Sale of a motor vehicle on hire purchase

Estoppel (s.21(1))

If the seller or buyer, by his conduct, makes the other party believe that a certain fact is true, and the other party alters his position, then he will later be denied (estopped) from saying that the fact is untrue. For example, this has arisen where a party has, for complicated reasons involving refinancing deals, signed a statement that his own property belongs to someone else and then ends up 'buying back' their own property. They may be estopped from denying the statement they made falsely about the ownership of the property (Eastern Distributors Ltd v Goldring).

The doctrine essentially deprives a person of their normal legal rights because of their irresponsible behaviour. They have allowed a false impression to be gained by another person who will suffer as a result if the doctrine were not applied. An early example (Pickard v Sears) involved a farmer who allowed a neighbour to borrow some of his equipment. The neighbour proceeded to enter negotiations with a third party for its sale. Despite discovering these negotiations, the farmer made no attempt to intervene. It was only after the third party had bought the equipment that the farmer insisted on its return. The court held that the farmer would be estopped from claiming his normal rights (repossession as the true owner) because of his irresponsible behaviour.

To be claimed successfully, estoppel can only be raised against a person who had actual knowledge of the facts and actually agreed to them knowing that a third party may rely on the 'apparent authority'. Clearly, misrepresentation is always involved with the doctrine.

Sale by a Mercantile Agent (s.2 Factors Act 1889)

A mercantile agent is one 'having in the customary course of business as such agent, authority either to sell goods or to consign goods for the purposes of sale or to buy goods, or to raise money on the security of goods (s.1 Factors Act 1889). So, for example, where the third party as a consumer buys a car from an agent who is in the car trade, this provision may apply.

The Factors Act 1889 states that the owner is bound by the actions of a mercantile agent in the following circumstances:

If the agent has possession of the goods, or the documents of title, with the owner's consent, any sale, pledge or other disposition of them in the ordinary course of business is as valid as if expressly authorised by the owner.

In *Folkes v King*, a car was sold by a dealer at below a stipulated minimum price. It was held that the sale was valid, that the buyer was therefore entitled to claim ownership, and that the only claim available to the seller was against the dealer for breach of warranty of authority. The buyer must however be innocent of the lack of authority of the agent at the time of sale. In *Pearson v Rose & Young*, the owner of a car took it to the dealer and asked him to obtain offers. The owner did not intend to hand over the registration book, but left it with the dealer by mistake. The dealer sold the car with the book to an innocent buyer. The question of the true ownership of the car was raised. It was held that the dealer had obtained the car 'with the consent of the owner' but this consent did not extend to the registration book, hence the sale must be treated as a sale without registration book and the buyer could not get good title to the car.

The agent must have received possession of the goods in their capacity as agents for sale – not in some other capacity such as for repair. In the latter situation, any sale of the goods would not be valid and the goods could be repossessed by the original owner.

Sale under a Voidable Title (s.23)

If the seller has a voidable title to goods and his title has not been avoided at the time of sale, the buyer acquires a good title to the goods, provided he did not know of the seller's defect of title.

Lewis v Averay

L. sold a car to a rogue, who resold it to A. L had been persuaded to accept a cheque from the rogue by his pretence to be Richard Greene, the well-known film actor. This was a misrepresentation and made the contract voidable. If L had taken steps to cancel the contract with the rogue before the car had been resold to A, he would have been able to repossess it. However, as the resale had already taken place, A was protected under s.23 and could keep the vehicle.

Because of difficulties of locating rogues in order to cancel the original contract it has been held, in the case of cars, that notifying the police amounts to avoidance of the contract (*Car & Universal Finance v Caldwell*)

Sale by A Seller in Possession (s.24)

A contract of sale can be complete and valid even where the goods are still in the possession of the seller (s.24), e.g. awaiting delivery. If in this situation, the seller sells the goods to a second buyer, the second buyer will obtain a good title to those goods if delivery of them is taken. However, the goods must be taken in good faith and without notice of the original sale. This leaves the first buyer in the position of having to sue the seller for breach of contract.

In *Pacific Motor Auctions Ltd v Motor Credits (Hire Finance) Ltd*, a car dealer sold a number of vehicles to the claimant under a 'display agreement'. This allowed the seller to retain possession of the cars for display in their showroom. He was paid 90% of the purchase price and was authorised to sell the cars as agents for the claimant. The seller got into financial difficulties and the claimant revoked its authority to sell the cars. However, the dealer sold a number of them to the defendant who took them in good faith and without notice of the previous sale. Whilst the defendant knew about the display agreement it was presumed that the dealer had the authority to sell the cars. As a result it was held that s.24 applied and that as the defendant had obtained a good title to the cars, the claimant would fail in their claim for the return of the vehicles.

Sale by a Buyer in Possession (s.25)

Disposition by a buyer in possession is a corresponding situation, where the buyer possesses the goods but the seller has retained property in them. Then, if the buyer has the goods and any necessary documents of title with the consent of the seller, and transfers these to an innocent second buyer, the latter will obtain a good title to the goods. Again, this is subject to the proviso that the second buyer takes the goods in good faith and without notice of any claims on the goods by the original seller (s.25). In *Cahn v Pockett's Bristol Channel Co* it was held that possession of a bill of lading with the owner's consent, was sufficient to pass good title to a third party under s.25. This provision is obviously significant where a reservation of title clause was part of the original contract of sale. A subsequent resale of the goods to an innocent second buyer may well be valid under s.25, although the position can be complicated and will vary from case to case. In *Worcester Works Finance Ltd v Cooden Engineering Ltd*, a finance company sold a car to a buyer (Griffiths) who paid for it by cheque. Griffiths then resold the car to another finance company under a hire purchase agreement. He remained in possession of the car. His original cheque bounced and the original owner cancelled the contract and repossessed the car. The second finance company brought an action against them, claiming that they owned the car and had a right to repossess. **HELD:** They could not recover the car - S.25 applied as the buyer was clearly a buyer in possession.

Sale of a Motor Vehicle under Hire Purchase (Part 3 Hire Purchase Act 1964)

There is a special protection afforded innocent private purchasers of cars sold when under hire purchase agreements. The innocent private buyer is able to claim ownership and can resist any claim by the finance company to repossess the vehicle. This protection does not apply to any other goods on hire purchase.

In Conclusion

- Transfer of title is concerned with whether (rather than when) ownership has passed – whether good title or a defective title has been transferred

- Problems can arise where a person without authority to sell proceeds to 'sell' goods to an innocent buyer

- Normally the original owner is protected under the Nemo Dat Doctrine (You cannot give a better title than the one you yourself possess) and will be able to insist on their return

- In order to encourage commerce, a number of exceptions to the doctrine have been created – in each case the innocent third party buyer is protected and will be able to keep the goods

- The main exceptions are estoppel, sale by a mercantile agent, sale under a voidable title, sale by a seller in possession, sale by a buyer in possession and sale of a motor vehicle under hire purchase.

Chapter 13
Non-Contractual Liability

In the absence of a contract on which to base a claim, it may be necessary to resort to alternative legal actions found either in the law of tort (in particular, negligence) or in statute (especially the Consumer Protection Act – Part One). These claims tend to be more difficult to bring successfully for a number of reasons, some of which are identified below. The chapter covers:

- Doctrine of privity of contract
- Contracts (Rights of Third Parties) Act 1999
- Collateral contracts
- Negligence liability
- Civil liability under Part One of Consumer Protection Act 1987 (CPA)
- Criminal liability under Part Two of the CPA 1987.

The most straightforward claim available to an injured party will usually be one for breach of contract. If he/she had purchased the faulty goods or substandard services directly, an action based on contract imposes strict liability on the supplier. There are, however, circumstances where the injured party has not entered into a contract with the organisation that caused the problem. Examples include purchasers of construction work where subcontractors have performed work incompetently, and passengers in a car which has been manufactured with design weaknesses and has crashed. Claims against the subcontractor or car manufacturer cannot be based on a normal contract action – the victim has not entered into a contract with them. The doctrine known as '**privity of contract**' operates – only the parties to a contract can claim rights based on the contract. The leading case illustrating this doctrine is:

Dunlop Tyre Ltd v Selfridge & Co

Dunlop sold tyres to a distributor on condition that they would not be resold at any subsequent stage of the supply chain at below the list price (this case was decided long before competition legislation banned such resale price maintenance). The distributor sold them to Selfridge who offered to sell them to the public at below the list price. **HELD:** Dunlop were not a party to the contract between the distributor and Selfridge and therefore had no rights to claim for an infringement of one of its terms.

The doctrine of privity of contract has led to considerable hardship or commercial inconvenience where, for example, exclusions from liability or indemnities in favour of third parties could not be enforced directly by the third parties involved. However, the doctrine has been modified by the passing of the **Contracts (Rights of Third Parties) Act 1999** which came into force on 11th May 2000. It also brings English law more into line with other systems of contract law.

The Act defines a third party as a person who is not a party to a contract. It gives a third party a right to enforce a contractual term in two situations:

- Where the contract expressly provides that he may;
- Where the term 'purports' to confer a benefit on him, unless on a true construction of the wording, it appears that the parties did not intend such a right of enforcement.

It is perfectly legitimate for the contract to contain a clause excluding the right of third parties to enforce its terms. The 1999 Act does not compel the contracting parties to grant enforceable rights to third parties. The Unfair Contract Terms Act cannot therefore be used to attack such an exclusion.

The third party must be expressly identified in the contract, although it is sufficient to fall within an identified class, or within the terms of a particular description. The Act gives the third party the same rights to obtain damages, an injunction, or order for specific performance as if it had been a party to the contract. It is possible to assign (transfer) the right to another organisation.

Specific Examples

In construction or building projects, the original parties (developer, contractors, consultants) may wish to encourage subsequent buyers or tenants by providing them with independently enforceable rights to complain about construction or design defects. It also permits contracts between a main contractor and sub-contractors to contain clauses enabling direct claims to be brought by the client against subcontractors for defective performance.

Firms passing on information in confidence will often allow the recipient to pass on that information to other people (e.g. advisors) subject to subsidiary confidentiality agreements being signed. The new law can permit direct enforcement for any infringement of these later agreements.

A franchisor may wish to have the ability to take direct action against sub-franchisees for breach of the franchise agreement made between them and the head franchisee.

Subject to the above reform, liability in these situations has traditionally been based on alternative rights provided by the law. These include:

- The finding of a Collateral Contract
- Negligence Liability from the law of Tort
- Statutory Liability based on the Consumer Protection Act 1987 (Part 1).

Non-Contractual Liability

Collateral Contracts

This involves the court discovering an implied contract, running parallel to the main one. It will be based on assurances given by a third party and which encourage the injured party to enter into a subsequent contract with a separate organisation. The assurances prove false and lead to damage being suffered. Examples include representations made by salesmen prior to a customer obtaining goods on hire purchase. The contract is actually made between the customer and a finance company to whom the goods have been sold by the dealer in the meantime. If those representations prove false and it leads to damage (which includes financial loss), the courts have held that a collateral contract exists between the dealer and the customer, allowing a claim for damages. Another example of collateral contract is the case of:

Shanklin Pier v Detel Products Ltd

The owners of the pier needed it to be repainted and consulted the defendants on paint which would be suitable for this purpose. The defendants assured Shanklin that a particular brand which they manufactured would be suitable and would last for at least 7 years. On this basis, Shanklin engaged contractors for the work and required them to use the paint recommended by Detel. The work was done competently, but within months, the paint began to peel badly. No action could be brought against the contractors in these circumstances. A claim was brought against Detel instead. **HELD:** In addition to the contract for the sale of paint, there was a second collateral contract between the claimant and Detel by which the latter guaranteed the suitability of the paint in return for the pier company specifying that the painters used it.

In the context of construction work and subcontractors, it will be advisable wherever possible to obtain a collateral warranty from the subcontractor. This provides the purchaser with a form of guarantee regarding performance of the work and entitles him to bring a direct contractual claim based on the warranty. However, some form of payment in return, even if only nominal, is necessary to satisfy the requirements of consideration.

Negligence

Within the civil branch of the English legal system there exists a body of rights and duties known as the law of tort. Tort actions are not based on rights provided by documents (such as the law of contract or trusts), nor on status (such as family law). These rights have been created predominantly by the courts and apply to the ordinary citizen and protect him or her against such wrongs as defamation, trespass, nuisance and deceit. However, by far the most important tort action is negligence. It covers a diverse range of situations, including accidents on the roads, at work and on other people's property. It is important to realise that tort claims in general, and negligence claims in particular are more difficult to win because they require proof of blameworthiness – it is fault-based liability unlike breach of contract which is strict liability.

The foundations of the modern law of negligence were laid in 1932 in the landmark case of:

Donoghue v Stevenson

Two women went into a café. One ordered some ginger beer and brought it back with two glasses. The bottle, which was made of dark, green glass, was opened and the glasses filled. Later, the glasses were refilled and, at this stage, the decomposed remains of a snail fell out of the bottle. Her friend suffered shock and severe gastro-enteritis as a result. Not having bought the bottle herself, she could not pursue a claim against the café-owner for breach of contract. She was advised to claim against the manufacturer in negligence – a test case, claims against a manufacturer by a consumer not having been brought before. **HELD:** The manufacturer owed a duty of care on the facts and had failed to take reasonable care. She was entitled to succeed.

Donoghue v Stevenson is a landmark case because it created the ground rules for establishing liability in negligence across the entire spectrum. The three essential ingredients for a successful claim are:

- A duty of care owed by the defendant to the claimant
- Breach of that duty
- Consequent damage.

Duty of Care

Lord Atkin created a new test to decide in what situations a duty of care is owed. He said that such a duty is owed to your 'neighbour':

> "You must take reasonable care to avoid acts and omissions which you could reasonably foresee would be likely to injure your neighbour. Who then in law is my neighbour? ... any person so closely and directly affected by my act that I ought reasonably to have them in contemplation as being so affected when I am directing my mind to the acts and omissions which are called in question."

This test has been refined over the years and a three stage test now operates:

- Was the harm caused reasonable foreseeable?
- Was there a relationship of proximity between the defendant and the claimant?
- In all the circumstances is it just, fair and reasonable to impose a duty of care?

The number of neighbour relationships has expanded dramatically since 1932 and covers many situations. We shall need to consider the position in three specific situations:

- Claims by purchasers against subcontractors
- Claims by purchasers against professionals (architects, surveyors, accountants etc.)
- Claims by consumers against manufacturers.

Subcontractors

The duty of care is relatively straightforward between purchasers and subcontractors. Most instances of damage caused to a firm employing subcontractors would be reasonably foreseeable to the subcontractors; there would be a sufficient degree of proximity between the two; there would be no clear reasons justifying the exemption from liability on grounds of public policy.

Professionals

The leading case relating to professional negligence liability is:

Hedley Byrne and Co v Heller and Partners

In this case it was held that a duty of care is owed by persons who occupy a special relationship of trust i.e. where what they say will be relied upon significantly by the person receiving the advice. This applies most obviously to advice provided by professional persons such as architects, valuers, surveyors and accountants. This enables claims to be brought by injured parties who have relied on negligent advice and suffered economic loss. Clearly, where the advice was given as part of services rendered under a contract for services, the client's most likely claim would be one for breach of contract, either based on an express term agreed between the parties to this effect, or an implied term that the work must be done competently (s.13 *Supply of Goods & Services Act 1982*). However, there may be liability in tort if a third party can prove reasonable reliance on the advice and that the defendant should have foreseen this reliance:

Yianni v Edwin Evans and Sons

Surveyors acting for the building society valued a house at £15,000 and as a result the plaintiffs were able to secure a mortgage of £12,000. The house was in fact suffering from severe structural damage and repairs were estimated at £18,000. The basis of the plaintiff's claim was not only the surveyor's negligence but that he ought reasonable to have contemplated that the statement would be passed on by the building society to the plaintiff and that they would rely on it, which they did. It was held that a duty of care was owed by the defendants. An important factor was that the price of the house indicated that the plaintiff was of modest means and would not be expected to obtain an independent valuation and who would in all probability rely on the defendant's survey, which was communicated to them by the building society. The court was also confident that the defendants knew that the building society would pass the survey to the purchasers and that they would rely on it.

Manufacturers

The authority for establishing liability of manufacturers to consumers of their products is *Donoghue v Stevenson* itself. Lord Atkin, after defining the neighbour test, went on to apply it to the case in question and made the following statement:

> "...a manufacturer of products which he sells in such a form as to show that he intends them to reach the ultimate consumer in the form in which they left him with no reasonable opportunity of intermediate examination, and with the knowledge that the absence of reasonable care in the preparation or putting up of the products will result in an injury to the consumer's life or property, owes a duty to the consumer to take that reasonable care."

There is no limit to the type of goods covered by this rule. Cases have involved goods as diverse as cars, a pair of underpants and a hot water bottle. Since 1932 the rule has been extended from manufacturers to cover anyone who does some work on the goods, for example, a repairer. The word "consumer" has been given a wide interpretation to cover anyone who is likely to be injured by the lack of care. In one case, a successful claim was brought by a pedestrian who was injured when a wheel from a vehicle which had been badly repaired became detached and careered along the pavement.

Breach of Duty

Having established the existence of a duty of care, the second requirement is for the claimant to prove a breach of this duty - probably the most difficult problem for him to address. This means that the claimant must be able to prove that the defendant failed to act reasonably in all the circumstances. In determining whether he has acted reasonably, the courts engage in a cost-benefit analysis in which they consider a number of factors. These include:-

■ The obviousness of the risk

- The likelihood of injury/damage
- The potential seriousness of the injury/damage
- The cost/practical difficulties in taking further preventative measures.

Liability in negligence is fault based and the onus of proving that the defendant was at fault is on the claimant. This can be very particularly difficult in claims against manufacturers as usually the consumer has no means of knowing exactly what went wrong in the manufacturing process. Sometimes, however, the only reasonable explanation for the defect is that someone acted negligently: buns, for example, do not usually have stones in the middle of them. In this kind of situation, the consumer may be able to plead **res ipsa loquitur** - the facts speak for themselves. This has the effect of reversing the normal burden of proof; the manufacturer is presumed to have acted negligently unless he can prove that he took all reasonable care.

To summarise

Breach of Duty

Standard of Care

to do what a reasonable man would do or not do what a reasonable man would not do

Factors to take into Account

- Obviousness of the Risk
- Likelihood of Damage
- Potential Seriousness of Damage
- Cost and Practical Difficulties of Doing More

i.e. a cost benefit analysis

Burden of Proof   claimant must prove case

on balance of probabilities

Exception   Res Ipsa Loquitur

                             (The facts speak for themselves)

Damage Resulting From the Breach

Even if breach of duty is established, the claimant still has to prove he has
suffered consequent damage. This requires him to prove that the damage
was caused by the defendant's negligent behaviour – that the damage
would not have been caused but for his behaviour (the "but for' test). If the
damage would have resulted irrespective of the defendant's actions, there
is a break in the chain of causation and the claim would fail. Where the
damage is partly the result of the defendant's actions and partly the result
of the claimant's actions, the court will allow the claim but reduce the
damages awarded – by apportioning blame in percentage terms and
reducing the figure by the blame apportioned to the claimant.

The damage suffered must have been reasonably foreseeable at the time
of the alleged infringement – it must not be too remote. Similar (but not
identical) principles apply here as with claims for damages in breach of
contract actions.

There are however some important restrictions on the type of damage
that can be claimed in negligence actions. Physical injury and damage to
property can be claimed, but economic loss is generally not claimable This
covers loss of profits and lost business. The authority for this position is:

Simaan General Contracting Co v Pilkington Glass Ltd

Goods supplied to the claimant by subcontractors were not up to
specification and a negligence action claiming economic loss was brought.
HELD: Claims for economic loss could only be made in very limited
circumstances.

The case of *Junior Books Ltd V Veitchi Co Ltd* suggested that where a
purchaser has 'nominated' a sub-contractor (a common practice in
building contracts), there is an ability to sue the sub-contractor for
economic loss. This was justified on the grounds that the two parties were
in closer proximity to one another, establishing a quasi-contractual

relationship. The position is however unclear and the Veitchi case has been extensively criticised.

A case illustrating the limits to claimable loss is:

Spartan Steel & Alloys Ltd v Martin & Co

The claimant manufactured steel alloys 24 hours a day. This required continuous power. Workmen, digging a trench in a public road nearby, damaged a power cable which resulted in a lack of power for 14 hours. There was a danger of damage to the furnace so this had to be shut down. As a result, one batch of molten metal was spoilt. **HELD:** Damages could be awarded for the value of the spoilt metal and the loss of profit caused to that melt (i.e loss based upon physical damage). However, the claimant's claim for loss of profits for the entire period of interruption was dismissed as pure economic loss and too remote.

The Consumer Protection Act 1987

For a number of reasons, including a European Directive requiring a reform, UK law introduced legislation in 1987 designed to provide stronger protection to consumers in relation to defective products. There was a recognition that the evidential problems of proving negligence in claims against manufacturers were often insurmountable and claimants either gave up or accepted settlements that were far below appropriate levels of compensation. The Consumer Protection Act 1987 contains several parts – Part One concerns civil law and the rights of individual consumers to pursue claims against manufacturers of defective products. Part Two et seq are more concerned with regulation of product safety and involve intervention by public authorities and the use of criminal sanctions to deal with abuses.

The main reform was to introduce a form of strict liability into product liability. All that the claimant had to prove was that damage has been caused to him as a result of a defective product which had been produced by the defendant. It was not necessary to prove that the defect had been caused by the defendant's negligence. However, because of intense lobbying by various industrial interests in the UK, strict liability was diluted by the drafting of a 'developmental risks' defence to such claims (see later).

Part One

Section 2 (1)

Liability arises :-

"where any damage is caused wholly or partly by a defect in a product"

The claimant must prove :-

a) the product was defective

b) the defect caused the damage or injury

Who is liable?

1) the producer (including component manufacturers, end product manufacturers, producers of raw materials)

2) the own brander (eg. Marks and Spencers - St Michael)

3) an importer into the European Union

4) any supplier who cannot identify his source of supply

Liability of a component manufacturer and an end-product manufacturer is joint and several - the consumer can sue one or both - each is fully liable for the damage

When is a Product Defective? (Section 3)

- "when the safety of the product is not such as persons generally are entitled to expect"

- definition very similar to that of "unsatisfactory " with the word "safe" substituted for "fit"

- however it does make clear that goods must be dangerous (not just defective) before rights are available

Relevant factors include:

■ the manner in which the product has been marketed

■ its get-up

■ any instructions or warnings provided.

If safer products are subsequently developed, their existence cannot be used as the sole reason for judging a product to be defective

Defences (Section 4)

1) that the defendant did not supply the goods (eg. manufacturer of finished product can be said not to supply component parts)

2) that the defendant did not supply the goods in the course of a business with a view to profit

3) that the defect was not present at the time he supplied it

4) the "developmental risks defence"

   ie. given the state of scientific and technological knowledge at the time when the product was put into circulation, no producer could have been expected to have discovered the defect. This is a particularly controversial defence and makes claims against firms in industries with close links with science and technology much more difficult eg. pharmaceutical companies

5) that the defendant was a component part producer and the defect was wholly attributable to its design or to compliance with instructions given by the producer of the finished product

Damages (Section 5)

Damages are recoverable for death and personal injury, including disease or other impairment of a person's physical or mental condition

Damages are recoverable for damage to other property

Cannot claim for loss or damage to :-

■ the product itself

- commercial property
- property claims of less than £275.

Limitation of Action

- The injured party must bring claim within 3 years of cause of action arising.
- The supplier cannot be sued more than 10 years after date when product supplied

Part Two

This part of the Act imposes criminal liability on firms which manufacture unsafe products. The Secretary of State can issue safety regulations providing more detail on how to satisfy the basic statutory duty (this has already been done for a range of items including furniture and children's night-clothes. Section 10 establishes the criminal offence of 'supplying consumer goods which are not reasonably safe.' The Secretary of State can serve a 'prohibition notice' on a supplier, prohibiting him from supplying goods which are unsafe or a 'notice to warn' which requires the supplier to publish warnings about the unsafe goods.

Further regulation relating to unsafe products was created by the passing of the General Product Safety Regulations 1994 as part of a European Union initiative to improve safety standards

In Conclusion

- As a general rule, contractual claims are easier to win because they are based on strict liability
- Problems arise where no contract exists between the injured party and the organisation responsible for the damage – the doctrine of privity of contract denies third parties a right to sue for breach
- The *Contracts (Rights of Third Parties) Act 1999* has created 'potential' inroads to the doctrine

- A collateral contract (implied contract running parallel to the main contract) can sometimes be identified, giving a contractual claim on the basis of an assurance received

- Negligence actions are from the law of tort and fault-based – it is necessary to prove that the defendant was to blame (culpable) for the damage.

- There are three ingredients to a successful negligence claim – a duty of care, breach of duty and consequent damage

- The modern law of negligence was founded in the case of *Donoghue v Stevenson*, which created the neighbour test for identifying duty of care situations

- Breach of duty is determined using a cost benefit approach, weighing the degree of risk involved against the costs of doing more than is already being done

- Consequent damage does not normally extend to economic loss

- The *Consumer Protection Act 1987 (Part One)* introduced a form of strict liability to claims involving defective products which have caused damage

- This 'strict liability' was weakened by the 'developmental risks' defence allowed in the Act

- Part Two of the *Consumer Protection Act 1987* imposes criminal liability on organisations manufacturing unsafe products.

Chapter 14
Agency and Assignment

This chapter covers a couple of miscellaneous issues relating to contracts and third parties.

Agency involves using another person or organisation to act on your behalf and possess the power to bind you to contracts negotiated with third parties. This can be achieved 'externally' where, for example, an organisation employs a commercial agent to sell its goods abroad or an employment agency to provide it with temporary staff. It also applies 'internally', where employees represent the organisation and make contracts on its behalf e.g. sales or purchasing staff entering into deals in the course of their employment.

Assignment involves the transfer of contractual rights and/or obligations to a third party after the contract was first concluded. The chapter covers the following legal principles:

- Agency – types of authority (actual, apparent)
- Ratification
- Doctrine of undisclosed principal
- Relevance of the Commercial Agents (Council Directive) Regulations 1993
- Rules relating to assignment of contractual rights and obligations
- Types of assignment – legal, equitable and by operation of law
- Novation

Agent's Authority to Bind the Principal

If an agent enters a contract with a third party and the contract is within the scope of his actual authority (express or implied), the principal is bound by the contract.

If the agent acts outside his actual authority but within the scope of his apparent authority, the principal is once again bound by the contract. Apparent authority is that authority which a third party would reasonably assume the agent to have in the circumstances involved.

If he acts outside his actual and apparent authority in making the contract on the principal's behalf, the principal is not bound by the contract unless he chooses to ratify it. For the principal to ratify the contract the principal must have the capacity and be identifiable at the time of the contract, the act must be capable of ratification and ratification must take place within a reasonable time.

If the agent contracts with a third party on behalf of his principal (where he is acting within his authority) but he does not make it clear to the third party that he is acting for the principal (the undisclosed principal), the principal is still permitted to enforce the contract against the third party who is unaware of his identity. This is despite the fact that the third party did not intend to contract with the principal. However, this will not be possible if the terms of the contract are incompatible with agency e.g. where the agent's personality is central to the performance of the contract. In cases where there is an undisclosed principal, the third party may choose whether to enforce the contract against the agent or the principal.

Commercial Agents (Council Directive) Regulations 1993

Since 1994, the above regulations have been in force and form a statutory code governing the activities of commercial agents (as defined). Essentially, a commercial agent is an agent engaged on a continuing basis to negotiate contracts for sale or purchase of goods. This precludes agents involved in services contracts and agents appointed on a one off basis to conclude a contract. The Regulations considerably strengthen the position of a commercial agent by implying terms into agency agreements and by giving rights which survive the termination of the agency agreement. They provide, for example, that the agent is entitled to compensation if the agency agreement is terminated and the agent is deprived of commission that he would have received if the agency agreement had been properly performed. Many of the statutory provisions cannot be excluded by express terms between the parties.

Contractual Assignment

A contract consists of rights and obligations. The general principle is that rights (the benefit being obtained from the contract) can be freely assigned (transferred). However, they must be proprietary and not personal to the original parties to the contract. Contracts in the publishing and recording industries are generally personal and cannot be assigned.

Contractual obligations (the burden) cannot be assigned without the agreement of the other party. This is designed to protect the party to the transaction who should not be prejudiced by a change in the identity of the person who has obligations under the contract. Sub-contracting the performance of the obligations is possible since the original party to the contract remains liable for the performance of his sub-contractor. To avoid this happening an express prohibition on sub-contracting is sometimes included in the contract terms.

There are three forms of assignment – legal, equitable and by operation of law:

- A legal assignment must be in writing and signed by the assignor; absolute (that is, of the whole interest and unconditional), and express notice must be given in writing to the other party or parties to the agreement (section 136, Law of Property Act 1925)

- An assignment that does not meet with the requirements of section 136 is an equitable assignment (provided there is a clear intention to assign). No particular formalities are required for an equitable assignment. The main difference is that an equitable assignment requires the assignee to join the assignor in any action under the contract.

- Assignment by operation or law arises on the death or bankruptcy of one of the parties where all the rights and obligations of that party pass to his personal representatives or trustee in bankruptcy.

Novation

A novation is a three way contract which extinguishes a contract and replaces it with another contract in which a third party takes up the rights and obligations which duplicate those of one of the original parties to the agreement.

Novations commonly arise on asset sales where the vendor wishes to assign all his rights and obligations under a contract to the purchaser. As contractual obligations cannot be assigned without prior agreement, the vendor can only achieve his aim if both the purchaser and the third party agree to a novation. The consent can be express (oral or written) or implied – where a customer, having received communication of the change of ownership, subsequently pays an invoice submitted by the new owner.

Take-overs and mergers will produce a similar need for novation. The identity of one of the parties to existing contracts will have changed and there is a consequent need to obtain consent to this change.

In Conclusion

- Agents are used as intermediaries to represent organisations and conclude contracts on their behalf
- Agents can be external to the organisation (specialist agencies) or internal (employees purchasing or selling goods for the organisation)
- Agents must possess the authority to act on behalf of their principal
- Authority can be actual (express, implied) or apparent (that which a reasonable third party would assume exists in the circumstances)
- Assignment involves the transfer of rights and/or obligations under a contract to a third party

■ Assignment of contractual rights does not require the consent of the other party whereas the assignment of contractual duties requires this consent

■ Novation is an extreme form of assignment and involves the replacement of the original contract by a new one under which the rights and duties of one of the parties have been assumed by another organisation e.g. upon a take-over or merger.

Chapter 15
Competition Law

Competition law has proved itself to be one of the most dynamic legal topics in recent years. The European Community provisions relating to cartels and abuse of a dominant market position have been subject to a number of significant amendments. Our own UK law on competition has been radically overhauled since 1998, bringing us into line with the EC approach. Some differences still exist, especially in the area of monopolies and mergers. This chapter covers the following issues:

European Regulation

- Underlying principles of EU competition law
- Article 81 (regulation of cartels) – ingredients for infringement
- Horizontal and vertical agreement – difference in approach to enforcement
- Exemptions (block and individual)
- Market analysis – approach
- Article 82 (regulation of abuse of dominant market position) – ingredients for infringement
- Case law examples
- Enforcement procedures.

UK Regulation

- Competition Act 1998 – changes to previous position
- Chapter One prohibition
- Chapter Two prohibition
- Exclusions and exemptions
- Procedures for enforcement
- Monopolies and mergers – Enterprise Act 2002
- Regulatory bodies – roles and responsibilities.

Reform of Competition Law

The Competition Act 1998 introduced the most radical changes to UK competition law for more than a quarter of a century.

Was this change necessary?

Critics of the UK approach to regulation of competition abuses point to the track record. It was estimated that cartels were adding up to 10% on prices of both industrial and consumer goods. Overall it was estimated that the cost of anti-competitive practices and abuse of market power amounted to about 1% of GDP – in other words, several billion pounds.

It has been argued that the main weaknesses of the U.K approach were a lack of bite in enforcement (inadequate powers of investigation coupled with weak penalties) and poor drafting of the main legislation which often concentrated on the form of agreements rather than their economic significance.

What has been the solution?

It was decided to adopt, with minor variations, the regime operating across the European Union for abuses that affect trade between member states – in particular the provisions found in Articles 81 and 82 of the European Treaty (formerly Articles 85 and 86 before ratification of the Treaty of

Amsterdam). This was partly an on-going process of harmonisation intended to free up barriers to trade between member states. However, it was generally recognised that the European model was far more effective in suppressing abuses. Although it has its critics (which led to recent proposals for reform) it possessed stricter controls both in terms of powers of investigation and enforcement of sanctions against abuses.

Continuing Reform

U.K. competition law was further reformed with the passing of the *Enterprise Act 2002*. This repealed the *Fair Trading Act 1973* and brought the approach relating to monopolies and mergers closer to the one used for anti-competitive practices under the *Competition Act 1998*. The *Enterprise Act 2002* also 'criminalised' cartel activities by making it possible for individual directors and managers to be prosecuted for their involvement in the illegal practice. This follows the U.S. policy and clearly in intended to have additional deterrent effect.

Future reform of the European Union policy on competition law includes the abolition of the present system of notification, exemption or clearance of restrictive agreements as required under Article 81 of the European Treaty. It is being replaced by a system of self-regulation where businesses will be expected to assess their own position and decide if there is a potential infringement of competition law provisions. With the expansion of the European Treaty as a result of the *Treaty of Nice*, the European Commission will also be transferring a significant amount of its competition law work to the domestic enforcement agencies of individual member states. In this country, it will be the Office of Fair Trading that will be dealing with the delegated work.

European Community Approach

The basic purpose of European Union competition policy is:

- to encourage free trade between member states;

- to break down barriers which inhibit such free trade;
- to ensure commercial undertakings do not prevent, distort or restrict competition or abuse their position in the market to the detriment of their competitors and/or consumers.

Articles 81 & 82 attempt to apply the above principles by setting out a body of detailed prohibitions and procedures.

Article 81

Regulates " all agreements between undertakings which have the object or effect of preventing, restricting or distorting competition."

Article 82

Regulates unilateral action by undertakings, prohibiting abuses of a dominant position

In addition, the **Merger Regulation** (Regulation 139/2004) attempts to deal with the issue of potential abuse by 'concentrations' being created within the common market.

Article 81

Article 81(1) prohibits all agreements between undertakings, decisions by associations of undertakings and concerted practices which may affect trade between member states and which have as their object or effect the prevention, restriction or distortion of competition within the European Union.

Article 81(2) states that such agreements are automatically void.

To infringe Article 81 requires a degree of **collusion** between **independent undertakings**, an **impact** of trade which **applies to more than one country** within the common market and either an intention or a consequence of **impeding competition** in a market.

Undertakings includes limited companies, partnerships, sole traders, trade associations and public utilities operating in commercial markets. Subsidiary companies are treated as part of the group and their holding company i.e. as one entity. Thus, agreements made between these companies would not be subject to Article 81 which requires 2 or more independent undertakings.

Companies which are based outside the European Union will still be subject to Article 81 if the consequences of their agreement affect trade within the common market.

Agreements have been interpreted widely and covers written and oral, formal and informal (gentleman's agreement), decisions of trade associations which may be no more than recommendations to be observed by members, and concerted practices. 'Concerted practice' has been defined as a form of co-operation between undertakings which, without having reached the stage where an agreement properly so called has been concluded, have knowingly substituted practical co-operation for the risks of competition. Some active contact needs to have taken place e.g. discussions or exchanging of information. Parallel behaviour is strong evidence of a concerted practice but not conclusive.

Effect on Trade between Member States

It is possible for agreements between businesses located in only one country, and which only operate in that country, to infringe Article 81. The ECJ has decided that such agreements can have the effect of encouraging the partitioning of the common market along national lines, which clashes with the overall policy of the European Treaty – that of removing barriers to intra-state trade.

Object or Effect of the Collusion (Anti- competitive practices)

The following examples (non-exhaustive) of prohibited agreements or practices is provided in Article 81(1):

- Directly or indirectly fixing purchase or selling prices;
- Limiting or controlling production;

- Dividing markets or sources of supply;

- Applying dissimilar conditions to equivalent transaction with other parties;

- Imposing supplementary obligations which have no connection with the subject of the contract involved.

Specific Examples

Directly or indirectly fixing purchasing or selling prices:

- Fixing the components of a price

- Setting a minimum price below which prices are not to be reduced

- Establishing the amount or percentage by which prices are to be increased

- Establishing a range outside which prices are not to move

- Indirect fixing includes arrangements relating to:

  - Discounts or allowances to be granted

  - Transport charges

  - Payments for additional services

  - Credit terms or the terms of guarantee

- Adherence to published price lists

- Consultation with potential competitors before quoting a price

- Not charging less than any other price on the market.

Sharing markets or sources of supply:

- Collusive tendering ("bid-rigging")

- Agreements between purchasers as to with whom they will deal

- Agreements between sellers by which they boycott certain purchasers

- Exchange of price information leading to price co-ordination and elimination of competition (information on pricing policy, discounts, costs, terms of trade, rates & dates of change

- Applying dissimilar conditions to equivalent transaction with other parties

- Aggregated rebates – the granting of better terms to a customer the more business he places with all the parties to the scheme.

These prohibitions apply to both horizontal and vertical agreements. Horizontal agreements occur when firms at the same level of trade are the parties e.g. agreements between two manufacturers or between two distributors. Vertical agreements occur when firms which are at different levels of trade are the parties e.g. between a manufacturer and a distributor.

Vertical agreements are generally seen as less of a threat to competition policy and are treated somewhat more leniently, although they can still fall foul of Article 81:

Consten & Grundig v Commission (EC)

A German manufacturer of TV sets and tape recorders etc. established an exclusive dealing network for the distribution of its products throughout the European Union. In 1957 G. appointed Consten as exclusive distributor in France. G. agreed not to sell directly or indirectly to anyone else in France; G's other national distributors were bound not to sell outside their allotted territories – so they could not sell in France; And C. agreed not to deal in competing products nor to sell outside France.

UNEF and other French firms managed to import G's products into France and undercut C's prices. C. sued these parallel importers in French law for 'unfair competition.' The validity of the exclusive distribution agreement was challenged as an infringement of Article 81 (then Article 85).

HELD: Article 81 was infringed to the extent that the agreement's aim of securing absolute territorial protection for C. against parallel imports partitioned the European Union along national frontiers, thereby distorting competition. It gave rise to different prices for the same goods in different member states.

"Appreciable Extent"

Article 81 does not apply to agreements which have a minimal effect (de minimus) on the market i.e. insignificant collusions. This is partly a recognition that some agreements are simply not worth pursuing because of their lack of impact and partly a recognition that the European Commission has limited resources to monitor every instance of collusion. Guidance is provided by the Commission in the 'Notice on Agreements of Minor Importance' (OJ 1997 C372/4).2 It makes a distinction between horizontal and vertical agreements and indicates that for the former, where the aggregate market share of the parties does not exceed 10%, the agreement will not contravene Article 81. A more tolerant minimum is then indicated for vertical agreements, set at 15%. There are some 'hardcore' exceptions though:

- Horizontal agreements which fix prices or limit production or sales, or involve market sharing;

- Vertical agreements which fix resale prices or allocate geographical territory to particular businesses.

An example of the de minimus doctrine in operation is *Volk v Vervaeke*, where an exclusive dealership agreement escaped violation of Article 81 because the total market share involved amounted to 0.2%.

Exemptions

The Commission has been given the power to exempt agreements, either on an individual basis or according to the category of agreement (the block exemption). Essentially, this has the effect of granting an immunity to the agreement, which otherwise would have been void under Article 81. There is also a process known as negative clearance, whereby the Commission, if requested by the parties, can declare that the agreement does not infringe Article 81 at all.

In order to obtain an exemption it is necessary to prove that the agreement/practice:

- contributes to improving production and distribution of goods and promoting technical progress;
- allows consumers a fair share of the resulting benefit;
- provided it does not enable the firms to eliminate competition in the relevant product market.

Examples of improvements in production or distribution are:

- lower costs from longer production or delivery runs
- lower costs from changes in the methods of production or distribution
- improvements in product quality
- increases in the range of products produced.

Examples of promoting technical or economic progress are:

- efficiency gains from economies of scale or increased specialisation in research and development
- increased pace of innovation as a result of shared R&D.

If the agreement leads to faster development of new products, new markets or to better distribution systems, the resulting benefits will be felt by the consumer. This would satisfy the second requirement above.

Relevant Market

An analysis of the relevant market to which the agreement relates has to be carried out by the Commission. It attempts to identify the potential boundaries of competition and therefore the relative size and strength of the parties to the agreement (and that of their competitors).

Two basic concepts are used in the analysis:

- Relevant product market
- Relevant geographical market.

Relevant product market involves identifying all the products/services which can be regarded as readily interchangeable or substitutable by the consumer. Relative characteristics, price and intended use are all relevant in arriving at a conclusion. These substitute goods would be included in the market if they would prevent prices of the products relevant to the investigation from rising above competitive levels.

Relevant geographical market involves identifying the territory in which the parties to the agreement carry on business in competitive conditions which are sufficiently similar and yet clearly differ from those operating in neighbouring areas.

Market Analysis

Relevant Product Market
Relevant Geographical Market

Product Market

Identify all readily Substitutable Products

- Characteristics
- Price
- Intended use

Demand Substitutability

Supply Substitutability

Ease of Entry into Market

Geographical Market

Identify the Territory

- Sufficiently similar competitive conditions
- Clearly different from neighbouring areas

Once the relevant market has been defined, the Commission can then decide whether exemption is appropriate.

Exemption can be either on an individual or a block basis. Individual exemptions require formal notification of the agreement to the Commission and all the attendant paperwork and problems of disclosure

For these reasons, firms usually try to fit the agreement within a block exemption which does not require such notification. This may not be easy, the agreement having to fit within the correct class and the terms be acceptable according to defined and detailed criteria. The following are the most important examples of block exemptions:

vertical agreements	Regulation 2790/1999/EC
research and development	Regulation 2658/2000/EC
specialisation	Regulation 2659/2000/EC
technology transfer	Regulation 772/2004EC
motor vehicle distribution and servicing	Regulation 1475/1995

The whole area of block exemption has been criticised as being over-formal and legalistic. There is pressure to make decisions on exemption more related to the economic implications/consequences of the agreements and less on the form in which the agreement is drafted on paper.

If it seems impossible or over-complex to fit the agreement within the boundaries of a block exemption, it may be necessary to seek individual exemption. Apart from the problems already mentioned (paperwork; disclosure of confidential information) there could be a lengthy period of investigation with no guarantee of formal exemption. Limited resources mean that the Commission gives a formal decision in less than 10% of applications. For the remainder, a 'comfort letter' is the likely outcome unless it has grounds for objection. Although such comfort letters will be regarded by the Commission as binding on its own future actions (unless new information comes to light which will affect its view on the matter) they are not binding on the courts when asked to decide on validity under Article 81.

Article 82

Once an undertaking has reached a dominant position in a given market, it becomes subject to regulation by Article 82. Dominance on its own is not an infringement but its abuses are:

> "Any abuse by one or more undertakings of a dominant position within the common market or in a substantial part of it shall be prohibited as incompatible with the common market."

There is no possibility of an exemption from Article 82, unlike Article 81.

Dominant Position

The essence of dominance is the power to behave independently of competitive pressures.

The classic definition of dominant position was provided in *United Brands v Commission*:

> "... a position of economic strength enjoyed by an undertaking which enables it to prevent effective competition being maintained on the relevant market by giving it the power to behave to an appreciable extent independently of its competitors, customers, and ultimately, of its consumers."

The same criteria are used to decide dominance as were seen applied to Article 81 – an economic analysis of the relevant product and geographical markets. Key indicators are:

Market share

There is a general presumption that a 50% market share amounts to occupying a dominant position. However, each case will be considered on its own merits and dominance has been held to exist even where the market share falls below 50%. In *United Brands*, the share amounted to between 40-45% but dominance was established.

Time

Dominance requires that a position of power has existed over a sufficiently long period of time.

Barriers to entry

The extent of potential competition will be a consideration, with the economic and financial difficulties involved in entering the market being examined e.g. how much capital investment would be needed?

Examples of barriers are:

- Intellectual property rights such as the need to obtain licences or permits.

- Preferential access to important inputs such as denial of access to the only port available for a particular market.

- The presence/size of sunk costs - highly competitive market conditions will make sunk costs more likely and thus deter entry.

Barriers to entry tend to be more prevalent in static markets rather than dynamic ones which are highly innovative.

Conduct

The actual pattern of behaviour of a company (its track record) can provide significant evidence of a position of dominance e.g. discriminatory pricing or selective distribution.

Another factor influencing dominance of a supplier in a market is the extent of buyer-power in the market. If there are relatively few buyers this could affect the ability of an dominant supplier to abuse its position.

Abuse of a Dominant Position

Simply occupying a position of dominance does not, it itself, amount to an infringement of Article 82. There must be an abuse of that position. Article 82 provides a non-exhaustive list of abuses:

- imposing unfair prices (or other unfair trading conditions);
- limiting production, markets, technical developments;
- applying dissimilar conditions (discriminatory);
- imposing unconnected supplementary obligations e.g. tie-in sales.

Article 82 is concerned with market structure and the effect it has on the level of competition. It is realised that where an undertaking occupies a dominant position in a market it will be able to weaken competition by manipulation of its influence in that market, and thus de-stabilise normal competitive practices.

Examples of Anti-Competitive Behaviour

These include expelling or excluding competition from a market.

Selective Distribution	where a manufacturer supplies only a limited number of retailers who must satisfy specified conditions (exclusive distribution involves supplying only one retailer).
Exclusive Purchasing	where the retailer agrees to purchase, or deal in, goods from only one manufacturer.

Tie-in Sales	where the manufacturer makes the purchase of one product (the tying product) conditional on the purchase of a second (tied) product (a set of tied products is called a bundle).
Full-line f orcing	an extreme form of tie-in sale where the retailer must stock the full range of the manufacturer's product range.
Quantity Forcing	where the retailer is required to purchase a minimum quantity of a certain product.
Fidelity Discounts	where the retailer receives discounts based on the proportion of its sales which come from the manufacturer.

Case Law Examples

(The original cases were decided when the relevant Article numbers were 85 & 86. Since ratification of the Treaty of Amsterdam 1997, they have been re-numbered 81 & 82. The case details below use the current Article numbers.)

United Brands v Commission

UB were charging different prices in 6 different countries for identical bananas. The ECJ held that this pricing policy infringed Article 82(c) [discriminatory pricing] because it amounted to an artificial price differential which distorted trade between member states.

N.B. The agreements with their distributors could also have been declared an infringement because they prohibited parallel importing from low to high price countries. This amounts to a restriction of trade between member states.

Hugin v Commission

Hugin were manufacturers of cash registers and new spare parts for their registers. Lipton was a distributor repairer of these machines. Hugin terminated the distribution agreement for what amounted to a minor infringement by Lipton and refused to supply it with spare parts in the future. The ECJ held that, although there was a highly competitive market for the supply of cash machines, Hugin had a dominant position in the separate market for Hugin spare parts and was found to be abusing it.

N.B. Hugin is frequently cited as authority for the proposition that Articles 81 & 82 can only be applied when the alleged abuse affects trade in more than one member state. In Hugin, it only related to part of the south east of England. This would not however prevent the domestic laws of the affected country from being used to deal with an abuse.

Tetra Pak v Commission 1997 (Tetra Pak II)

Tetra Pak required purchasers of its machines to agree to a range of support facilities (spare parts, maintenance and the purchase of its own cartons). This prevented other firms who produced cartons capable of being used in the machines from competing in the relevant market. The ECJ held that this was an abuse of Article 82(d). Tetra Pak were fined 75m Euros.

Articles 81 and 82 – Enforcement by the European Commission

The Commission possesses wide powers of enforcement of Articles 81 and 82. Complaints can be made by businesses affected by the alleged infringement and by member states. The Commission can also initiate action itself. The following powers exist:

- To demand information relevant to an investigation.

- To search premises.

- To take copies or extracts of records.

These powers have been largely adopted under the *Competition Act 1998* for investigations by the Director General of Fair Trading into infringements which operate only inside the UK. We shall look at the powers in more detail when considering the new Act.

Apart from ordering an agreement or practice to be declared void, the Commission may also, by decision:

- Require a company to terminate any infringements resulting from the agreement

- Order the parties to refrain in future from similar conduct (*Polypropylene Cartel, 1986*)

- Order the parties to inform interested parties that the infringement has been brought to an end (*Tetra Pak II,* 1992)

- Order the parties to make information periodically available to the Commission (*United Brands,* 1976).

The Commission's main weapon, however, is its power to impose fines where companies have intentionally or negligently breached the articles. The following page provides some further detail on this sanction.

Penalties

- The Commission can impose fines of up to 10% of the total turnover in the previous year of each of the undertakings concerned or 1 million Euros, whichever is the greater.

- Failure to terminate an infringement can result in continuing fines of up to 1000 Euros per day.

- Fines of up to 1000 Euros per day can be imposed against undertakings which :

  - refuse to provide information requested by the Commission, or

  - refuse to co-operate in the course of an investigation.

All Commission decisions, including decisions to investigate, enforcement decisions and details of fines imposed, will be published. This can clearly have serious repercussions on the business involved in terms of business reputation and standing.

Recent Examples of Fines

Computer games company Nintendo was fined   149m in November 2002 for seeking to prevent parallel imports of its game from the UK (where they were 65% cheaper) to other EU states where they could be sold by parallel importing companies at a higher price

The European Commission fined Sotheby's   20.4m for a seven year price fixing arrangement with their main auction-house competitor, Christie's. The latter was given total exemption from any fine because it had come forward and exposed the activity to the Commission (whistleblowing). The fine was equal to 6% of Sotheby's annual turnover.

In May 2004, the European Commission fined Microsoft close to   500m for bundling its media player software with its Windows operating system. This represented abuse of a dominant position in the pc market.

The Competition Act 1998

What is the New Act Achieving?

It brought UK law into line with EC competition law by adopting a very similar approach, principles and procedures to those found in Articles 81 & 82 of the European Treaty.

To do this it was necessary to abolish a number of UK Acts which previously governed the position:-

- Restrictive Trade Practices Act 1976
- Restrictive Trade Practices Act 1977
- Resale Prices Act 1976
- (Substantial parts of) the Competition Act 1980.

The monopolies and mergers provisions found in the Fair Trading Act 1973 (FTA) continued to apply until 2003.

The Act came fully into force in March 2000, but a number of transitional arrangements began to apply from 1998. One of the first changes to be brought into effect under the Act was the abolition of the Monopoly & Mergers Commission and its replacement by the Competition Commission (CC). The latter continues to carry out the investigative role previously held by the MMC on monopolies and mergers but with enhanced powers

There are two sets of provisions dealing with anti-competitive practices:

Chapter One Prohibition   (Section 2)

This is essentially concerned with anti-competitive agreements between independent undertakings within a market (cartels etc.). These used to be governed by the Restrictive Trade Practices Act 1976 as amended.

Chapter Two Prohibition   (Section 18)

This focuses on abuse by one undertaking (occasionally by more than one acting in concert) of a dominant position within a market. Previously, UK law in this area had been governed by the Competition Act 1980 (and by the FTA 1973 where the dominant position amounted to a monopoly as defined).

Chapter One Prohibition

The approach and content of Article 81 of the European Treaty are closely followed. The same position is taken relating to:

- Definitions of agreement (including decisions and concerted practices)
- 'Appreciable effect' on competition
- Specific examples of infringements e.g. price fixing, market sharing cartels, bid-rigging, resale price maintenance)

'Appreciability' will be determined by reference to the combined market share of the undertakings involved. The same market analysis will be used to decide the 'relevant market' (product market, geographical market etc.). However, the Office of Fair Trading (OFT) will generally consider a combined market share of less than 25% to lack the 'appreciable effect' required for an infringement. However, if the agreement relates to any of the following hardcore abuses, it will be potentially an infringement even if it falls below the 25% threshold:

- market-sharing, price fixing, resale price maintenance or a network effect caused by the cumulative impact of several smaller agreements

There is no requirement to notify the OFT of agreements which lack an appreciable effect on the relevant market.

Exemptions

The same criteria for granting exemption apply as for Article 81. It is possible to obtain exemption under the Competition Act in any of the following ways:

- Individual exemption by the OFT
- Block exemption on a UK basis
- Parallel exemption based on Article 81(3) of the European Treaty.

Individual exemptions require prior notification and approval. Block exemptions automatically apply without the need for notification. Parallel exemptions do not apply where the European Commission has merely issued an informal comfort letter. However, it is unlikely that the OFT will disagree with the Commission's view on a request for individual exemption.

For a short time, under UK law, vertical agreements were excluded from the provisions of the Competition Act 1998. However, this was seen to be too significant a departure from the European Treaty approach of allowing them exemption, subject to the usual requirements. They are now covered by a block exemption.

Chapter Two Prohibition

Again, the same basic approach and content found in Article 82 is adopted, including the list of non-exhaustive infringements (excessive or predatory pricing, refusal to supply, applying dissimilar terms to equivalent transactions etc.).

As a general rule, the Competition Act presumes a market share of 50% or above involves a position of dominance within that market.

Where the undertaking holds less than 40% it will be presumed not to have such a position unless special factors make it unusual.

Conduct of Minor Significance

Where the dominant undertaking engages in conduct of minor significance (based on UK turnover) it will not reach the appreciability threshold and will not be subject to fines. It need not notify the OFT of the conduct.

Exemptions

There are no exemptions permitted (consistent with Article 82) and the limited exclusions apply only to horizontal restraints.

Powers of Investigation

Under the Competition Act the Office of Fair Trading has the following powers:

- To require production of specified documents or specified information (s.26).
- To enter premises without a warrant (s.27).
- To enter and search premises with a warrant (s.28).

The Office can investigate activities only if it has reasonable grounds for suspecting an infringement of either the Chapter One or Chapter Two prohibitions.

What can provide evidence to create reasonable suspicion?

- Copies of secret agreements
- Statements from employees or former employees
- A complaint by a rival business.

These can trigger the formal powers of investigation. There is nothing to prevent the Office obtaining information through informal enquiries e.g. through written correspondence, over the phone or at meetings. Although firms are encouraged to co-operate, the Office does not possess statutory powers when carrying out such informal contact and cannot force responses.

Powers to Require Production of Specified Documents and Information

The Office can require the production of relevant material and stipulate when and where it must be made available. This includes such material as:

- invoices
- sales data
- agreements
- minutes of meetings
- diaries of specified personnel.

It can require the content of specified documents to be explained at a meeting arranged for this purpose. An example would be technical data which includes codes. The instruction to provide the specified material can apply to any organisations connected to an alleged infringement, not just those under suspicion. Therefore, complainants, suppliers, customers and competitors can be ordered to provide documents or information.

The Office can take copies or extracts from any document produced. It has the right to see records held on computer e.g. invoices or sales figures.

Power to Enter Premises Without a Warrant

The OFT has power to carry out on-site investigations where he has the same reasonable grounds for suspicion we identified above. Normally, two days written notice must be given to the occupier of the premises but this can be dispensed with :

■ If the premises involved were being occupied by the party under investigation (or there were reasonable grounds for suspecting this), or

■ The investigating officer has been unable to give notice to the occupier, despite all reasonable steps

Upon entering the premises, the investigating officer possesses the same powers as were identified above for the production of specified documents.

'Premises' does not include domestic premises unless the home is used partly for business purposes. It does include any vehicles used by the business.

The occupier must be informed in all cases of his right to have a legal adviser present. A short period of time will be allowed for a legal adviser to be contacted and arrive on the premises. Such delay will be kept to an absolute minimum because of the risks of evidence being tampered with or other organisation being alerted. Certain security measures can be imposed in the meantime. These include the sealing of filing cabinets, closure of external e'mail systems and the restriction of movement of key personnel involved. If there is an in-house legal adviser, no such delay will be allowed.

Power to Enter and Search Premises
with a Warrant

A High Court judge can issue such a warrant where there are reasonable grounds for suspecting the presence of documents on the premises involved:

■ which the OFT had previously required to be produced either by written request (s.26) or in the course of an on-site investigation without a warrant (s.27), and which have not been produced; or

- which, had the OFT required their production under s.26, would have been concealed, removed, tampered with or destroyed; or

- which could have been required by the investigating officer in a previously attempted on-site investigation where he was refused entry.

The officer can use reasonable force (but no more) in an effort to gain entry to the premises, but not against any person who may resist.

The usual powers operate once entry has been obtained, including taking copies. He can also take possession of documents where it appears to be necessary for preserving the documents or preventing interference with them (or where it would not be reasonably practicable to take copies). Where originals are taken, which would be exceptional, they must be returned within three months.

Documents/Information which Can Be Withheld

Organisations can refuse to produce 'privileged communications' i.e. those between a professional legal adviser and his client or those made in connection with legal proceedings. Professional legal advisers includes in-house lawyers such as those employed in an organisation's legal department.

There is also a defence against self-incrimination which means that the OFT cannot compel the production of any document or information which might involve an admission by an organisation of the existence of an infringement. It will be for the Office to have to find evidence by other means.

Confidential information relating to an individual or specific business activities of an organisation should not be disclosed without the consent of the person who originally provided the information. If potentially confidential material has been required by the investigating officer, it should be clearly marked as such and put into a separate confidential annex

Enforcement

The Office has the following powers available for enforcement of the Act.

■ To issue directions to discontinue an infringement.

■ To issue interim measures whilst an investigation is being carried out.

■ To impose penalties in appropriate circumstances for an infringement of either Chapter One or Chapter Two.

Directions

The OFT has a discretion to issue appropriate directions to bring an infringement to an end. This could require a modification of the existing agreement or practice or its complete cessation. The direction (which could be addressed to a parent company of a subsidiary which has committed the infringement) could require further action to be taken. Examples include informing third parties of the cessation or periodically reporting back to the OFT on specified points.

There is a right to inspect the OFT file relating to the proposed direction (except for confidential information or the OFT's internal papers). An appeal is available against a direction and would be heard by the Appeals Tribunal of the Competition Commission. In the meantime, the direction would remain effective. The direction will be published on the register kept by the OFT and on a website on the Internet.

If necessary, the OFT can apply to the High Court for an order requiring compliance. This would be successful if an organisation is failing to comply without reasonable excuse and will require compliance within a specified time. Refusal to observe the order amounts to contempt of court and can result in fines and/or imprisonment. Additionally, court costs will have to be paid by the organisation(s) in default.

Interim Measures

This administrative power (which did not exist before the Act) is designed to prevent serious damage being caused by the suspected infringement during the course of the investigation.

The damage can be either to other businesses or to the general public. This includes the possibility of a smaller competitor being put out of business in the immediate future or where a competitor is suffering from a considerable competitive disadvantage.

The interim measures can require an agreement to be terminated or conduct to be discontinued or for them to be modified.

Penalties

From 1st March 2000, it has been possible for the OFT to impose a financial penalty of up to 10% of the UK turnover of the infringing organisation for each year of the infringement, up to a maximum of 3 years. This is a considerably heavier sanction than any previous fine available in the UK for breach of UK domestic competition law and brings the UK into line with the penalties available to the European Commission for breach of Articles 81 and 82. The severity of the penalty is partly intended to act as a deterrent to other organisations who may otherwise be tempted to engage in anti-competitive practice.

The track record of the organisation may prove relevant in deciding intention or negligence e.g. previous infringements of the Restrictive Trade Practices Act 1976 or the Competition Act 1980. It is no defence to plead ignorance of the technical requirements of the new law.

Where an organisation has participated involuntarily in an infringement e.g. by being a reluctant member of a cartel, it could still be found to have acted intentionally or negligently but have the penalty imposed against it reduced because of this mitigating factor.

Small Agreements and Conduct of Minor Significance

Provided the above do not relate to price fixing, there is an immunity from financial penalties for organisations which satisfy the relevant criteria for the above concepts: These will be defined by UK turnover figures. This immunity applies only to penalties however. The agreements can still be declared void and third parties can still sue for damages.

Guidance on Penalties

The OFT is required to publish guidance as to the appropriate amount for any penalty. The following sets out the framework for decisions on levels of penalties:

Step 1

Assess the gravity and duration of the infringement

Step 2

Assess whether there should be an increase based on aggravating circumstances, and if so, what level it should be

Step 3

Assess whether there should be a reduction based on mitigating circumstances, and if so, what level it should be

Step 4

Take into account a number of objective factors such as economic and financial benefits obtained by the infringing organisation

The presence of a suitably drafted compliance programme which is being effectively operated by an organisation is a mitigating factor which can reduce the penalty imposed.

Another mitigating factor applies to the case of whistleblowers who co-operate during an investigation into the existence of a cartel. This can result in either an exemption from financial penalty or a reduction in the fine imposed. The OFT will have regard to a Notice published by the European Commission in 1996 which relates to 'secret cartels between enterprises aimed at fixing prices, production or sales quotas, sharing markets or banning imports or exports.' In such cases, the Commission will seriously consider reducing the penalty or even granting exemption for undertakings that are prepared to provide information and co-operate in their investigation.

Although this only operates in relation to Article 81, the OFT is expected to follow the same approach in Chapter One cases.

Appeals

Appeals against the decision to impose a fine or against the level of a fine will be heard by the Competition Appeals Tribunal. The Appeal Tribunal can impose, revoke or vary the amount of a fine. A further appeal on the level of fine decided by the Tribunal can go to the Court of Appeal.

Recent Examples of Fines

Argos and Littlewoods were fined £22.5m for fixing the prices of toys and games

Ten companies including Manchester United and the Football Association were fined a total of £18.6m – the second highest fine imposed by the OFT – for a price fixing arrangement on team shirts.

Monopolies and Mergers

UK Position

The UK law on monopolies and mergers was significantly reformed in 2003 by the bringing into force of the Enterprise Act 2002. Amongst other matters not relating to competition law, the 2002 Act repealed the Fair Trading Act 1973 which had regulated monopolies and mergers since the 1970's. It was the one example of U.K. competition legislation that had not been abolished by the Competition Act 1998. What follows is a brief summary of its main provisions

Monopolies

Part Five of the Enterprise Act 2002 makes provision for a system of market investigations by the Competition Commission (a body that replaced the Monopolies and Mergers Commission in 1998 with enhanced powers). The purpose of these investigations is to inquire into markets where it appears that the structure of the market or the conduct of suppliers or customers is harming competition.

These market investigation references replace the earlier monopoly inquiries, and the Act repealed the relevant parts of the old Fair Trading Act 1973 that used to govern monopolies.

Making a Reference

The OFT may make market investigation references to the Competition Commission (CC). When making a reference, it must have reasonable grounds for suspecting that one or more features of a market prevents, restricts or distorts competition in relation to the supply or acquisition of goods or services in the UK (or part of the UK).

The OFT may accept undertakings in lieu of a reference from appropriate personnel in order to remedy the adverse effects on competition. In other words, the matter is resolved on a voluntary basis without the need to enter formal procedures involving the CC.

Competition Commission - Investigation and Remedies

A detailed investigation (with a maximum period of two years to complete) is carried out by the CC. If an adverse effect on competition is identified, the CC must decide how best to remedy the situation - either in the form of voluntary undertakings or compulsory orders. Orders could include requirements to modify existing trading arrangements, including a break up of the company structure into independent trading concerns.

Appeals

There is a new right to apply for a review of decisions taken by the CC (or the OFT) in connection with market investigation references. The case would be reviewed by the Competition Appeal Tribunal (CAT). The CAT is not allowed to substitute its own decision on the merits of the case, but can review the lawfulness and fairness of the decision and if necessary, require the CC or OFT to reconsider its decision.

Mergers

In the context of mergers and take-overs, UK competition law is now based on the Enterprise Act 2002.

Part Four allows proposed mergers to be subject to investigation if they would result in:

- the value of the assets taken over exceeding £70 m, or,

- a monopoly (25% or more of the relevant market)) being created

The OFT must consider (within a maximum period of four months) whether the merger may be expected to result in a 'substantial lessening of competition'. If the OFT believes that this test is, or may be, met, then it must either refer the merger to the Competition Commission (CC) or, if appropriate, seek undertakings from the merging parties.

If the merger is referred to the CC, it will conduct a full investigation to determine whether it will result in a substantial lessening of competition. It must complete its investigation within 24 weeks.

The Enterprise Act 2002 has made some significant changes to the previous position e.g.

- the Commission makes its own decisions, with no political involvement from the DTI

- the criteria has ceased to be based on public interest and become more competition-based – will the merger have the consequence of distorting competition within the relevant market - similar to the Competition Act 1998 approach for anti-competitive practices

The Commission has the power to prohibit the merger. Alternatively it could impose remedies in the form of undertakings which would be subsequently monitored by the OFT.

EU Position

The Merger Regulation (Regulation 139/2004)

Clearly, the merger of two or more undertakings within a market can have significant repercussions on trading practices and the level of competition that will continue to exist. Although the European Treaty does not itself regulate such 'concentrations,' Regulation 139/2004 requires notification of concentrations with a common market dimension.

'Concentrations' include take-overs and full function joint ventures.

Once notification has been received, the Commission has 3 weeks in which to decide whether an investigation is required and inform the parties (and the member states affected). If an investigation is carried out, a decision must be made within 3 months whether the proposed merger is approved. The basic question being asked is:

- Is the concentration creating a dominant position within a market which could impede effective competition within the common market?

Competition Law Institutions

The Office of Fair Trading

Established in 1973

Given statutory status in 2003 (Enterprise Act 2002)

Non-ministerial department of government

Main role – to protect consumers and to enforce UK competition policy

Governed by Chair & Board

Two main Divisions:

- Consumer Affairs Division
- Competition Policy Division

Both Divisions provide legal advice on competition legislation and publish a wide range of guidance literature

Competition Policy Division seeks to protect customers and suppliers by monitoring abuses of market power:

Monopolies

If potential distortion of trade within a market, OFT can refer 'monopoly situation' to Competition Commission for formal investigation or encourage voluntary undertakings from business involved. OFT can monitor subsequent activities of the organisation if the Commission has obtained undertakings.

Anti-competitive Practices

Using the new powers under the Competition Act 1998, OFT can investigate and take action where restrictive agreements or abuse of a dominant position can be identified. OFT can either seek voluntary undertakings, act under its own powers or refer matter to Competition Commission (see earlier material on new powers)

Resale Price Maintenance

Imposition of minimum resale prices to the public are unlawful except in highly unusual circumstances where it can be argued to be in the public interest (no continuing examples of such exceptions now exist). OFT monitors business markets to ensure compliance.

Mergers

OFT seeks to identify impending mergers (or ones that have already occurred). May seek voluntary undertakings from the undertakings concerned or refer the merger to the Competition Commission.

OFT liaises with European Commission and can be used to assist in investigations on European competition law infringements

* (For investigation powers and enforcement sanctions, see earlier notes)

The Competition Commission

Replaced the Monopolies and Mergers Commission (MMC) in 1999

Initially acquired an appeal function from decisions of the OFT. This responsibility was transferred to the newly formed Competition Appeal

Tribunal in 2003

Reporting function:

- Similar to the MMC pre 1999
- Based largely on Enterprise Act 2002 (replacing the Fair Trading Act 1973) and privatisation statutes
- Concerned with monopolies, mergers and regulatory inquiries
- Each inquiry will have 4 or 5 members of the Commission
- Time limits – normally 3 months for mergers or newspaper inquiries

- Time limits – maximum 24 weeks for mergers
  normally 6 months for a utility case
  normally 9-12 months for a monopoly inquiry
  (max of 2 years)*

Monopoly inquiries and merger inquiries are referred to CC by the OFT (occasionally by the Secretary of State for DTI)

Cannot initiate own inquiries

Power to make own decisions and use enforcement techniques

* it is anticipated that these will focus heavily on complex monopolies in future (Scale monopolies are effectively banned under the Competition Act 1998)

The Competition Appeal Tribunal

Created in 2003 by the Enterprise Act 2002

Consists of a President, panel of Chairmen, and ordinary members

Hearings will consist of Chairman and two other members

Functions:

Hearing appeals from decisions taken by the OFT or sectoral regulators under Chapter One or Chapter Two of the Competition Act 1998 with the power to confirm, set aside or vary the decision, or remit the matter to the

OFT or regulator

Hearing claims for damages where an infringement of competition law has been established under Chapters 1 or 2 of the Competition Act 1998 or Articles 81 or 82 of the European Treaty

Reviewing decisions on mergers or market investigation (monopoly) references taken by the OFT, Competition Commission or regulators

Further appeals proceed to the Court of Appeal and House of Lords

Department of Trade and Industry

Responsible for regulating and supporting trade and industry

Seeks to ensure fair standards of business practice

Seeks to protect consumer

Contains various agencies including Companies House and Patents Office

Divided into Directorates, including:

Corporate & Consumer Affairs

Corporate & Consumer Affairs

[company affairs including competition & fair trading

 company investigations

 consumer matters including consumer safety]

Above includes the Competition Policy Directorate

Objective – to create and maintain effective markets free of abusive practices

Can refer mergers to Competition Commission for investigation and decision

European Commission

See Page 129

In conclusion:

- Competition law concentrates on two forms of abuse – agreements between independent organisations to manipulate market conditions (cartels) and abusive behaviour by individual organisations in a dominant position

- UK competition is regulated by a combination of domestic and EU measures

- The UK approach to regulation is largely modelled on the European measures with some differences

- The main EU measures are Article 81 of the European Treaty (cartel regulation) and Article 82 (abuse of a dominant position)

- The main UK domestic measures are Chapter One of the Competition Act 1998 (cartels) and Chapter Two (abuse of a dominant position)

- The Enterprise Act 2002 now regulates the position on monopolies and mergers in the UK

- Definitions of collusion and dominant market position, criteria for exemption, analysis of market power, and enforcement techniques are largely identical between the EU and UK provisions

- The EU measures only apply when the abuse affects trade between member states

Chapter 16
Intellectual Property Rights

Intellectual Property Rights (IPR) cover a wide range of 'intellectual' assets based either on creativity (inventiveness) or on protection of existing reputation. Both have significant effects on competitiveness and business success, achieving or maintaining a cutting edge in the market or relying on a strong well-recognised image. Patents, design rights, confidentiality and copyright clearly relate to inventiveness whereas trade marks and the tort action of passing off relate to protection of reputation. IPR are vigorously protected by a combination of statutory and common law principles and by contractual terms and conditions.

The chapter covers the following legal issues:

- Justification of IPR
- Classification of IPR
- Remedies for infringement
- Patents - requirements of successful claim
- Patents – employee rights
- Trade marks – changes introduced in 1994
- Trade marks – requirements for successful application
- Trade marks – enforcement rights
- Trade marks – community trade mark
- Passing off – requirements for successful claim
- Passing off – case law

- Confidential information – requirements for successful claim
- Confidential information – basis of action (contract, equity)
- Confidential information – position of employees
- Design rights – classification (registered, unregistered)
- Design rights – requirements for successful application/claim
- Design rights – exclusions
- Copyright – changes introduced under the Copyright, Designs & Patents Act 1988
- Copyright – requirements for successful claim
- Contractual provisions relating to IPR

What are Intellectual Property Rights?

It is an area of law that concerns itself with legal rights connected with creative effort or commercial reputation and goodwill. The law attempts to deter other people or firms from either copying or taking unfair advantage of the work or reputation of another by providing remedies.

The main remedies involved are :

- Copyright
- Law of confidence
- Patent
- Registered design
- Design right
- Trade marks
- Passing off

Intellectual Property Rights (IPR) are 'property' in the legal sense. They can be owned, assigned or licensed. They belong to that category of property where rights can only be enforced by legal action (choses in action) as opposed to land and other tangible property where rights can be enforced by taking physical possession. Intellectual property is the most basic form of property – a man uses nothing other than his mind to produce it.

How are IPR justified?

A man should own what he produces – that which he brings into being. If what he produces can be taken away from him, he is 'no better than a slave'.

Strong protective laws should exist to encourage investment in research and development. This, in turn, increases general wealth, employment and prosperity.

The strong laws can be made a vehicle for the dissemination of new ideas and innovation by requiring their general publication in exchange for providing the protection. This facilitates the expansion of further R&D leading to yet more discoveries and innovation.

How can IPR be classified?

Some rights create monopolies; others merely prevent the unfair use by others of an existing work or article. Some rights require registration before they become effective (sometimes these are called hard IPR); others operate automatically without any need to register (soft IPR)

Some rights are based on legislation; others were formed by common law (judge-made)

HARD IPR	SOFT IPR	STATUTORY	COMMON LAW
Patents	Copyright	Patents	Confidentiality
Design right	Unregistered Design Right	Trade Marks	Passing off
Trade marks	Confidentiality	Registered Design Right	
	Passing Off	Unregistered Design Right Copyright	

Traditionally, most of the above rights (patents, trade marks, design rights) were known as industrial property. The more modern terminology (which includes copyright) is intellectual property rights. Some contracts will still use the older expression. If they do, they should clearly specify which rights are involved, especially with regard to copyright.

Why are IPR important in business?

In the international context there is a direct correlation between investment in research and development and competitive success. Compared with their competitors, Japan and Germany generally have higher levels of long term investment and awareness of the importance of innovation and the design process.

In the domestic context it is not surprising that the two largest manufacturing industries, chemicals and aerospace, also have the highest levels of investment in research and development. Such industries are highly competitive internationally. They contribute significantly to the nation's revenue and balance of trade, employ large numbers of workers and make considerable profits for their shareholders.

The impact on the consumer of the legal protection of intellectual property is enormous. Where products are protected by intellectual property, whether it be by patenting, reputation or trade marks, the manufacturer is able to charge a premium. Brand names in the fashion industry are an obvious example of this phenomenon. This trend is growing and many sizeable undertakings now find that the value of their IPR may well be significantly greater than their other, more tangible assets.

Remedies

The range of remedies available for infringement of IP rights are:

- Injunctions
- Damages
- Account of Profits
- Court orders for seizure of infringing articles etc.

Patents

Some Introductory Points

- Governed by the Patents Act 1977, which is based on the European Patent Convention
- A patent creates a statutory monopoly in an invention with the exclusive right to use/exploit it for up to 20 years
- After 20 years, the invention falls into the public domain and can be used by any competing organisation
- The justification for a strong patent monopoly is that it provides a reward to the inventor for effort, encourages innovation and enables

recovery of research costs, and is a form of payment for allowing the invention to be published and technological understanding improved in general

- Few patents last the full 20 years – they either fail to make enough money or they are overtaken by technological advance

- Most patents are created by employees working in teams for large companies – not by isolated geniuses (the mad boffin image)

- Patents are stronger than trade secrets because the monopoly continues even if the secret enters the public domain

Competitors may attempt to break a patent by:

- challenge (producing a similar product which is not covered by patent)

- invalidation (proving that the product/process was not new or did not involve an inventive step)

- infringement (larger organisations may risk court action in the belief that legal costs will intimidate smaller companies who hold the patent)

Techniques available to deal with (3) above include:

- Licensing a larger organisation with the resources to protect against infringement

- Arranging insurance cover

- Negotiating a licence with the potential infringer

Procedure

Patents require registration wherever protection is sought. There are clear advantages in multiple registration procedures where one application will cover a block of countries. An application for a patent can be made either to the European Patent Office in Munich or the British Patent Office in Newport. British applicants are obliged to file first in the U.K for reasons of national security.

Approximately 27000 new applications are made each year and around 180,000 renewals.

How long will an application take?

There is a timetable for processing applications with the maximum time limits indicated below:

Patent Applications

File Application   (Priority date)

Preliminary Examination and Search

Search Report

'A' Publication (18 months after priority date) :

- the application

- the search report   18 months

Substantive Examination

Grant and 'B' Publication   Maximum 4.5 years

Procedural stages

Filing

The date of the invention is the date when it is first filed ("priority date") Infringement proceedings can arise from this date

Publication

Within 18 months, the Patent Office must publish the application, allowing for public inspection. This is carried out by the government printer and is despatched world-wide.

Examination and Search

Within 6 months of publication the applicant should request that an examination and search be carried out. This involves a search through the relevant technical literature, including previous applications. Much of the material is now located on cd rom and other forms of electronic retrieval. The examiner will raise any objections and allow time for amendments. Claims are likely to be honed down during this process.

Grant of Patent

A final decision must be made within 4.5 years of the initial application. If it is granted, a notice must appear in the Official Journal (Patents) so that it has been officially published. The patent will last for 20 years subject to payment of the relevant renewal fees.

Who may make the application?

According the Patents Act 1977, the only person entitled to apply is the inventor. "Inventor" is defined as the devisor, but persons who possess property rights over the invention also can apply. This normally refers to the employer involved.

What are the contents of the application?

- Request for grant of a patent
- Specification containing a description of the invention
- Claim or claims defining the scope of the patent
- Abstract summarising above

Requirements for successful Application

Under s.1(1) of the Patents Act 1977, the following conditions are required for the grant of a patent:

- the invention is new (novelty)
- it involves an inventive step (obviousness)
- it is capable of industrial application

+

- the grant of a patent for it is not excluded (under the Act)

  Section 1(1)

  Patents Act 1977

Novelty

The Patents Act 1977 defines novelty for the first time. S.2(1) states that an invention shall be taken to be new if it does not form part of the state of the art. Under s.2(2) 'state of the art' is defined as all matter which, prior to the priority date, has been made available to the public, whether in the U.K. or elsewhere. Lack of novelty can be used as a defence to infringement proceedings (the 'Gillette defence') and can lead to revocation of the licence.

The question of novelty hinges on whether the invention has already been 'disclosed to the public'. This can be either through published documents (forming part of the state of the art) or through being known to the public (having been seen in operation).

Disclosure to a single individual can be sufficient. However, disclosures in breach of confidence will not be admissible.

Laboratory use and testing in secret does not undermine novelty.

Disclosure can take place even if the audience is unaware of its significance at the time

Windsurfing International v Tabur Marine GB

A patent had been sought for a navigational boom for a wind-surfer. It was established that an 11 year old boy had been seen using a crude prototype off the English coast in the 1950's. This defeated the application on the grounds of lack of novelty.

Obviousness (Inventive Step)

'Invention' is not defined but s.3 indicates an inventive step involves something that is not obvious to persons skilled in the art, having regard to any matter which forms part of the state of the art.

'State of the art' consists of all matter that has been made available to the public before the priority date.

Obviousness is determined in court by expert witnesses being examined and cross-examined.

In deciding obviousness the clearest modern test is found in the Windsurfing case. This four-fold test was restated in a more concise form in *Molnycke AB v Proctor & Gamble* :

- What is the inventive step alleged to be involved?
- What was the state of the art at the priority date?
- In what respect does the step go beyond or differ from the state of the art?
- Would the step be obvious to a skilled man?

However, a variety of tests have been used over the years. The commercial success of an invention has sometimes been proposed as a test of obviousness (although not a complete one – success could be the result of heavy investment in advertising). An early test which is still taken into account is whether the invention satisfied a 'long-felt want' – where the problem had waited solution for many years.

No one test will prove totally effective because of differing contexts and technological advance e.g. in the field of microbiological research. However, the Windsurfer test has resulted in a more standardised approach since its formulation.

Exclusions

A number of exclusions are found in s.1(2) and (3) of the Patents Act 1977 e.g. an application will not be accepted if the matter falls within the natural ambit of another intellectual property right.

The invention must be capable of industrial application e.g. discoveries and theories, ideas or mathematical formulae in the abstract cannot be patented. However, incorporation of a discovery into technology is patentable – a technical contribution to the art. It is the practical application of the idea or discovery that is needed.

Schemes, rules, methods for performing a mental act, playing a game or doing business, or a programme for a computer and the presentation of information are excluded. Occasionally, if a technical element is present, a patent can be obtained e.g. a method for arranging buoys for navigational purposes; a method for distributing utilities services on an housing estate; a method of teaching pronunciation of language combined with a reading machine (presence of a mechanical element)

Patent applications relating to medical treatment are not allowed. It is argued that no-one should have a monopoly on mechanisms which relieve human suffering (processes for medical treatment of human beings for the cure or prevention of diseases). Exceptions include a new method of contraception (pregnancy not being a disease) and new cosmetic treatments e.g. hair improvers (same argument).

Biological inventions are not patentable on ethical grounds – animals and plants should not be the subject of patents and monopoly practices. Exceptions can be found including the Onco mouse (which was developed for research leading to the improved treatment of cancer patients). However, microbiological processes and products may be patentable. Problems arise in distinguishing between biological and microbiological processes – no definitions have been formulated. One controversial area of current applications for patents relates to DNA sequences which have enormous implications for the future medical treatment of patients.

Defences to Patent Infringement Claim

A number of defences can be available to defendants in actions for infringement of a patent. The majority are contained in s.60 of the Patents Act 1977:

- Invalidity
- Licence
- Prior Use
- Exhaustion of rights
- Accidental Infringement
- Public Policy

Invalidity

Here the defendant will argue that the patent should be revoked. The challenge will be based on the requirements of s.1(1) on grounds of lack of novelty or inventive step. In essence it is arguing that the patent was granted in error and should be nullified (Licensees of a patent are unable to challenge on grounds of invalidity unless the licence specifically allows for this).

Licence

This is a complete defence. The alleged infringement must however come within the ambit of the licence in terms of duration (not after the licence has expired), geographical area (although this may cause problems for the licensor if the restrictions are seen to infringe competition law regulation as being anti-competitive), and extent of activities permitted (e.g. a licence to use does not extend to manufacture as well).

Licences can be implied as in the case of a licence to repair where the purchaser of a patented product gives the item to a third party for repair.

The purchaser of a patented product assumes ownership and will be entitled to re-sell it unless the original sale restricts this.

Exhaustion of Rights

Once a patented product has been put on the market in any EC country with the consent of the proprietor, the disposal will have exhausted his rights and no subsequent disposal will infringe.

Prior Use

A person cannot be restrained from continuing to do what has hitherto been done. If another firm has been working on parallel lines and can prove prior use, it turns the monopoly into a duopoly.

Accidental Infringement

The general principle is that it is no defence for the defendant to argue innocence. Infringement does not require fault on the part of the infringer. There are some exceptions though e.g. accidental or temporary entry of a foreign registered aircraft or vessel into the U.K.

Public Policy

If it can be shown that the alleged infringement was done for non-commercial purposes e.g. for education in private, experimental application, it will not infringe the patent.

Employee Rights

Under s.7, the applicant for a patent has to be its inventor. This is defined as its devisor or any person entitled to property in the patent. Where the invention is produced by an employee or employees working for a firm the employer will normally claim patent rights using the property argument above. This is usually based on express provision in the contract of employment, but even if the contract does not have a specific clause dealing with patent rights the courts have held that it contains an implied undertaking to hand over patent rights for inventions made during the course of employment. The invention is said to be held on trust for the employer under the employee's implied duty of good faith and fidelity.

Section 39 reinforces the rights of the employer. It states that any invention made in the course of employment shall belong to the employer where it was made:

a   in the normal course of the normal duties of the employee, or

b   in the course of duties falling outside his normal duties but specifically assigned to him, and in either case, an invention might reasonable be expected to result.

Section 40 allows employees to claim compensation where the employer has patented to invention and it has been of outstanding benefit. It allows employees to claim a fair share of this return. In fact, only a handful of such claims have been made since 1978.

Trade Marks

This section contains a description of the following features of trade mark law:

- Background to the Trade Marks Act 1994
- The new definition of a trade mark
- Powers of the Trade Mark Registrar to refuse registration
- Rights of a trade mark proprietor to bring infringement proceedings
- Defences to infringement proceedings
- Community trade marks

The Trade Marks Act 1994

This Act made radical changes to the previous law, improving rights of the proprietor. This was achieved in the following ways:

- Brought UK trade mark law into line with the rest of the EC
- Created a presumption in favour of registration
- Widened the definition of a trade mark
- Made registration of geographical names easier
- Overturned previous restrictions on registering shapes
- Extended rights to include marks on packaging
- Allowed three dimensional 'signs' to be registered
- Allowed colours to be registered
- Allowed smells and sounds to be registered
- Created a more flexible licensing system
- Created a number of new criminal offences
- Extended rights to complain about similar signs on dissimilar goods

Duration

Marks can be registered for an initial period of 10 years (previously 7) with renewal periods of 10 years (previously 14). This provides for consistency with EC law and the Madrid Protocol.

Definition of Trade Mark

Section 1(1) of the Trade Marks Act 1994 defines a trade mark as any sign capable of being represented graphically and capable of distinguishing the goods or services of one undertaking from those of other undertakings.

It further states that a trade mark may consist of words (including personal names), designs, letters, numerals or the shape of goods or their packaging. The mark must be used to denote the source or origin of the goods/services concerned. "A word or words, to be really distinctive of a person's goods, must generally speaking be incapable of application to the goods of anyone else. There must be some quality in the mark that earmarks the goods so marked as distinct from those of other producers of such goods.

Trade Marks

'Any sign capable of being represented graphically and capable of distinguishing the goods or services of one undertaking from those of other undertakings'

May consist of:

- Words (including personal names)
- Designs
- Letters
- Numerals
- Shape of goods
- Packaging
- Must denote source or origin of the goods/services

Refusal to Register

Under Part 3 of the Act it is the duty of the Trade Marks Registrar to maintain a register and scrutinise applications for trade marks. He must ensure that successful applications comply with the requirements of the Act and that owners of existing marks are protected. There are a number of absolute grounds for refusal to register found in section 3. e.g.

- if a sign does not meet the requirements of s1(1) of the Act (see above)
- if the mark is devoid of distinctive character (being merely descriptive)

Invented words are more likely to satisfy the second barrier, although problems can still arise here. In *SF & O Hallgarten's Application*, the word 'Whiskeur' was refused for a product that combined liqueur and whisky. It was regarded as merely descriptive of the product rather than a trade mark. The courts are cautious with invented words where they are attempting to get around the restrictions on the character and quality of the goods (again becoming descriptive). In the *Orwoola*, the court held that the mark was a misspelling of "all wool" and did not form a distinctive mark. This could in fact be misleading if the goods were not entirely made of wool. Misspelt words are not treated as invented, although a combination of two misspelt words may be seen to acquire distinctiveness.

Section 3 also allows for refusal if the mark would be contrary to public policy or morality. An example of such a refusal is *Hallelujah Trade Mark* where the name 'Hallelujah' was to be used to sell women's clothes.

Section 4 bans trade marks which consist of or contain a representation of a national flag of the UK if it appears to the Registrar that its use would be misleading or grossly offensive.

A mark which is applied for in bad faith or with no honest intention to use will be refused registration.

Refusal under Section 5

Any person is entitled to oppose an application for registration of a trade mark. This may be done by arguing that s.5 has been infringed. This permits the Registrar to refuse registration of a mark:

- which is identical or similar to a mark for identical goods;
- which is identical or similar for similar goods and there is a likelihood of confusion;

- which is identical or similar and is applied to goods which are dissimilar but the mark has a reputation.
- Where the opposition is based on similarity and confusion (2 above) the established test is as follows:

Is there a real likelihood of deception amongst a number of people between normal use of the previous trade mark registration and normal use of the proposed registration?

An example of a challenge under s.5 is *Portakabin v Portablast.* The totality of the impression was stressed with the sound as well as the visual appearance being relevant. As the first five letters in both words looked and sounded the same the application was rejected as the rest of the words did not diminish the initial impression. Some cases have suggested that similarity between the first two syllables of two words is of most significance in deciding the issue.

The nature of the target audience is taken into account – does it consist of experts and trade professionals or ordinary members of the public – consumers? However, the ultimate purchasers of goods are not presumed to be unusually unobservant. In *Morning Star v Express Newspapers* (1979) it was said that "only a moron in a hurry" could have confused the two titles.

Infringement Proceedings

The proprietor enjoys exclusive rights in a registered trade mark (s.9). It becomes part of his personal property and entitles him to bring infringement proceedings. Section 10 sets out the grounds for complaint i.e. where a mark has been used without consent which is:

- identical on the same goods for which the mark was registered; s.10(1)
- identical or similar on the same or similar goods where there is a likelihood of confusion; s10(2)

- identical or similar on goods which are dissimilar but where the trade mark enjoys a reputation, and use of the mark will be detrimental to its reputation. s.10(3)

The marks will be compared on a mark by mark basis. A case illustrating the approach is

Wagamama Ltd v City Centre Restaurants

The claimant had a successful Japanese restaurant in London under the registered trade mark 'Wagamama,' a Japanese word. The defendant, in April 1995, opened a restaurant in London selling Indian food under the name Rajamama. The court considered both the look and sound of the name in deciding there was an infringement under s.10(2).

Damage can take a number of forms where infringement has occurred. Confusion leading to wrong association with another company can affect issues such as the quality of goods sold, the type of business carried out, the ability to obtain credit and the inconvenience of confusion caused by suppliers making mistakes as to identity

In some situations it is a defence to infringement proceedings (or opposition to an application for registration) to argue concurrent existing use. In the latter case, this allows the Registrar to permit two identical marks to be registered. The Act provides that the Registrar shall not refuse an application because of an earlier trade mark unless objection for this reason is made by the earlier registered proprietor. If an objection is raised, however, it would appear that refusal is automatic [s.5(3) is relevant here – a trade mark cannot be registered for dissimilar goods if the previous mark has an established reputation]

What is honest, concurrent use?

The court will consider whether "there was really only some fictitious or colourable use and not a real or genuine use."

Community Trade Mark System

Under the "Harmonisation Directive," regulations have been passed bringing a common trade mark system into operation since April 1996. This enables a single application for registration to cover all member states of the EU. It provides protection across the 15 countries and the ability to enforce trade mark rights under the relevant legal system where the infringement took place. Very similar rules apply to granting registration as under the Trade Marks Act 1994.

The benefits of Community registration are the saving of time and money and the greater ease of enforcement if infringements take place. It also avoids having to identify slight but significant differences in registration requirements in individual member states. The significance of such registrations is bound to increase in time with the expansion of international markets.

A Community trade mark is renewed every 10 years and will be cheaper than multiple renewals in individual countries.

Passing Off

This section will provide you with a description of the following aspects of the law of passing off:

- Basic definitions of passing off
- Meaning of goodwill
- Meaning of 'get-up'
- Prospective goodwill
- Deception, not mere confusion
- Common field of activity
- Target audience
- Types of 'damage'
- Use of own name
- Future of passing off
- Additional cases

A trader must not"...sell his own goods under the pretence that they are goods of another man."

The essential elements of this common law action (an economic tort) were identified in Erven Warnink bv v Townend & Sons (Hull) Ltd as:

- A misrepresentation;
- made by a trader in the course of trade;
- to prospective customers or ultimate consumers of goods/services supplied by him;
- which is calculated to injure the business or goodwill or another trader; &
- which results in damage to a business or goodwill of a trader or is likely to do so.

(per Lord Diplock)

Another formulation was put forward in *Reckitt & Colman v Borden* (1990) by Lord Oliver. He suggested that passing off contains 3 elements:

- goodwill or reputation attached to the goods or services supplied with an associated 'get-up';

- a misrepresentation by the defendant to the public leading or likely to lead to the public believing that the goods/services offered by him are those of the plaintiff; &

- actual or likely damage by reason of the erroneous belief engendered by the defendant's misrepresentation.

Essentially, the tort consists of three ingredients – reputation (or goodwill) acquired by the claimant in his goods, name or mark; misrepresentation by the defendant leading to confusion; damage to the claimant.

Goodwill has been defined as "the attractive force which brings customers in." In actions for passing off, the claimant must prove that the goodwill is linked in the public imagination to a 'get-up' – a distinctive mark or name. An early example is **Birmingham Vinegar Brewery Co v Powell** where 'Yorkshire Relish' was a widely known sauce manufactured by the plaintiff. It had attained the necessary distinctiveness even though the precise identity of the manufacturer was not so well known.

Names, fancy or invented words, shapes and colours can all constitute a 'get-up'. In **Hoffman La Roche v DDSA** the defendants imitated the colouring of a specific brand of tranquilliser. This was held to be passing off, even though many people did not know the name of the specific manufacturer involved. The 'get-up' of the tablets had created in the mind of the public a particular source of manufacture.

Most cases involve names or invented words.

The goodwill may be limited geographically but, equally, it is possible for the trade to take place abroad. In **Maxim's Ltd v Dye**:

The claimant, an English company, owned a world famous restaurant in Paris known as 'Maxim's'. The defendant opened a restaurant in Norwich and also named it 'Maxim's'. It was held that the plaintiff had goodwill in England derived from the business in France which might be regarded as prospective. The claimant might want to commence trading in England in the future and should be able to rely on the goodwill he had in connection with the name.

Mere confusion in the mind of the public is not enough. There must be a degree of deception – a false representation, whether fraudulent or otherwise.

There must be a common field of activity between the plaintiff and the defendant.

Mccullogh v Lewis A May Ltd :

The claimant was a well known children's broadcaster who used the name 'Uncle Mac'. The plaintiff had some physical infirmities. The defendant sold cereal under the name 'Uncle Mac' with indirect reference to the claimant's infirmities without the claimant's permission. It was argued that the public might draw certain conclusions harmful to the image of the claimant e.g. that he was prepared to receive large payments for commercial advertising which conflicted with the image he had cultivated with the public.

HELD: The claim must fail as there was no common field of activity such as would cause confusion in the minds of the public. He was in public broadcasting. The defendants were in the manufacture and marketing of cereals (questionable reasoning here).

The same principle was applied in *Wombles Ltd v Wombles Skips Ltd* :

The claimant company owned the copyright in the books and drawings of the Wombles. Its main business was granting licences in respect of the characters; for example, it granted one such licence for waste paper baskets for children. The defendant formed a company to lease builders' skips. He decided to call the business 'Wombles Skips Ltd' because of their association with tidying up rubbish.

HELD: There was no common field of activity and therefore no danger of confusion (even allowing for the licence relating to waste paper baskets.)

Sometimes, however, the facts are less clear-cut and the decision more difficult to anticipate. In *Lego v Lemelstrich*

The well-known Lego company, which makes coloured plastic construction bricks for children, was granted an injunction preventing the use of the name Lego by the defendant who was planning to use it for its plastic irrigation and garden equipment. It was held that the name had become so closely associated with the claimant's business that there was a potential for confusion – the common field of activity in this case being coloured plastic.

For a claim to be successful, the claimant must show that a substantial number of the public are likely to be misled. The nature of the target audience needs to be taken into account (is it a professional audience or the general public?) However, the court will not have regard to unusually stupid people.

Proof of damage is essential – either existing or likely to be suffered. This can cover a range of matters including diversion of sales, damage to reputation, and even loss of a licensing opportunity.

An example of damage to reputation is ***Harrods Ltd v R. Harrod Ltd*** :

The claimant was a well known company with a banking department, but which was precluded from operating as a moneylender by the articles of association. The defendant registered a money-lending company under the 'fancy-name' of R. Harrod Ltd, that is a name having nothing to do with his own name. This fact together with his advertising style showed that he was acting fraudulently in an attempt to gain advantage from these similarities and the claimant was granted an injunction to restrain the defendant from using that name.

Placing secondary goods or inferior goods on the market, making out that they were the goods of the claimant amounts to damage to reputation.

Occasionally an action for passing off will lie through injurious association i.e. even though the plaintiff and the defendant are not in the same line of business, a false suggestion by the defendant that they were connected with one another could harm the reputation of the plaintiff's business. In ***Annabel's Club v Schock*** , it was held that there was a possibility of confusion between the plaintiff's night-club and an escort agency set up by the defendants using the same name.

Use of Own Name

No-one can claim copyright in a single word or name. It is however possible to restrain the use of a name under the law of passing off, subject to an exception – the right of a person to use his own name in business.

The right to trade in one's own name does not extend to the right to use it as a trade mark though if the result would lead to confusion.

Ultimately, the key question in each case seems to be whether the use of a name is calculated to deceive the public. Confusion in itself is not enough. English law does allow a person generally to use his/her own name honestly in the market, but not if it is being used intentionally to deceive and confuse the public. The intention behind the use of the name is therefore crucial to a claim for passing off here. In *Parker Knoll V Knoll International* (1962) Denning L.J. gave the example that a man called William John Pears cannot set up a soap business and call his soap 'Pears Soap'.

Future of Passing Off

An important feature of this tort is that its boundaries are never static. It moves with the times to accommodate new situations and problems. This can make accurate definition of the tort a dangerous activity. One example of recent development is *Lego v Lemelstrich* where, despite there being no apparent common field of activity, it was held that the claim would be successful and the damage included the loss of a licensing opportunity.

The widening of the definition of a trade mark in s.1 (1) of the Trade Marks Act 1994 may seem to make actions for passing off less important in the future. Firms can register a trade mark and receive statutory protection – a stronger and often easier basis of complaint. There are however a number of reasons why this common law action is likely to remain relevant to protection of trade marks. Some organisations, by their very nature, are unlikely to wish to go to the lengths of registering a trade mark e.g. charities and other voluntary organisations. They may however wish to protect their activities through an action for passing off. It also retains a relevance where the Registrar is considering applications for new trade marks. He is obliged, under the Trade Marks Act 1994 to consider the rights of proprietors of earlier unregistered marks and should not allow any marks which would infringe a passing off claim. Also, because of a number of uncertainties in the law of registered trade marks, it is always advisable to bring an alternative claim for passing off in addition to an infringement claim under s.10 of the 1994 Act. This would cover the problem if the trade mark were declared invalid or was revoked.

Additional Cases

Associated Newsagents v Insert Media Ltd

The defendant's business was to arrange advertising through inserting leaflets in newspapers. Without permission of the plaintiffs, they attempted to do this with a group of newsagents (the Daily Mail and Mail on Sunday were affected) **HELD** An action for passing off successful. The public would be confused and assume the inserts had the support and approval of the newspapers. There was a misrepresentation and a risk of loss of goodwill and reputation by the plaintiffs.

Bollinger v Costa Bravo Wine Co

"Spanish Champagne" declared an infringement. "Champagne" has to come from a particular part of France.

Erven Warninck v Townend

The claimant made advocaat (from eggs and spirits). The defendants started making an egg flip (from dried eggs and Cyprus sherry) but decided to call it advocaat because of the latter's success and popularity. **HELD**: A claim for passing off was successful. The plaintiffs had a considerable reputation to protect and the use of the same name for a product made from different ingredients was an infringement.

Confidential Information

The following section provides you with a description of the following aspects of the duty of confidentiality:

- Examples of confidential information
- Requirements for a successful complaint
- Definitions of 'confidential'
- Definitions of where the duty is owed
- Classification – contractual and equitable claims
- Employee obligations – express and implied contractual terms

Some of the classic examples of intellectual property protected by confidentiality are

- Coca Cola (coke)
- Chatreuse Liqueur
- Kentucky Fried Chicken
- Listerine Mouth Wash

Confidential information can include hi-tech processes, customer lists, prices and background financial information.

The duty applies to firms engaged in negotiations that may or may not lead to a contract, and to undertakings engaged in partnering agreements. It also applies to employees (and ex-employees for a limited time).

Breach of Confidence - Requirements

- The information must be "confidential"
- The disclosure must be where there was an obligation not to confide
- There must be actual or anticipated unauthorised use or disclosure.

1. Confidential Information

Confidential information has been defined as "something which is not public property or knowledge" (Lord Green in *Saltman Engineering v*

Campbell Co.). Another definition is found in *Thomas Marshall (Exports) v Guinle*. Sir Robert Megarry suggested there are 4 elements :-

i   the owner believes its release will be injurious to him;

ii   the owner believes the information is secret (not in the public domain);

iii   both beliefs are reasonable.

iv   the information must be judged in the light of the particular industry's usages and practices.

2.   Obligation Not to Confide

2 tests have been developed to help define the circumstances where the duty applies :-

i   The Reasonable Man Test;

ii   The Limited Purpose Test.

i   Would a reasonable man, in the shoes of the recipient, realise on reasonable grounds that the information was being given to him in confidence?

There is a strong presumption in favour of such a realisation in business circles.

ii   Was the information disclosed only for a limited purpose or purposes? If this is the case it should not be used for any other purpose. There is again a strong presumption in business circles that this will be the case.

Saltman Engineering v Campbell

The claimant owned the copyright in drawings of tools for use in the manufacture of leather punches. The defendant was given the drawings and instructed to make 5000 of the tools at 3s 6d each. After completing the order, the defendant retained the drawings and made use of them for its own purposes. **HELD:** There was an implied duty only to use the drawings for the limited purpose of producing the 5000 punches. The defendant had infringed this obligation of confidence.

Fraser v Thames Television

The claimant had disclosed in confidence to a television company an idea for their own show. When the company tried to use the idea for a series featuring other actresses, without first obtaining the plaintiff's consent, it was held to be in breach of confidence.

Actions for Breach of Confidence

There are two possible ways to base a claim for breach of confidence:

i   Breach of Contract, or

ii   Equity

1   Breach of Contract

It can be covered either by an express provision in the contract (which will add clarity to what is being protected) or by an implied term relating to confidentiality. In *Thomas Marshall (Exports) v Guinle:*

The defendant was appointed as the managing director of the plaintiff company for ten years. His service agreement stated that he was not to become employed in any other business without the company's consent and that he must not disclose confidential information. Further, after ceasing to be managing director, he was not to use or disclose confidential information about the customers of the plaintiff company. When his service contract had another four and a half years left to run, he resigned. **HELD:** The defendant was not infringing the express provision in the contract which did not cover using the information in a business of his own. However, he was infringing the implied duty of fidelity and good faith owed to his employer and an injunction would be granted banning its continuation.

In Schering Chemicals v Falman;

The claimant was a drug company which manufactured a drug called Primodos. It had been suggested that the drug could have harmful effects on unborn children and as a result the company suffered bad publicity. It engaged the first defendant to train its executives in television techniques and to put across the plaintiff's point of view. The first defendant engaged the second defendant to help with the training courses. The plaintiff supplied a large amount of information about the drug to the first defendant which was in turn passed on the second defendant. It was acknowledged that the first defendant had received the information in confidence, but it was never established whether the second defendant gave a similar express undertaking to respect confidence. Shortly after the training course, the second defendant proposed to make a programme about Primodos for Thames Television. Much of the information in the programme would have been obtained from the training courses information, although most of it would have been available from other public sources. The drug company applied for an injunction to restrain the use of the information. **HELD:** The defendant was in breach of an implied promise to use the material for only one purpose – the training courses.

2   Equity

Sometimes information is disclosed during negotiations and no contract is concluded. Here the recipient may be subject to an equitable duty not to breach confidentiality. In *Coco v A.N. Clark (Engineers) Ltd:*

The claimant entered into informal negotiations with the defendant for the latter to manufacture a moped he had designed. These negotiations broke down but only after certain confidential information on the design had been disclosed. When the defendant decided to build its own engine to a design which bore a close resemblance to that of the plaintiff, Coco brought an action against it. He was not granted an injunction on the grounds that his case was too weak for this remedy to be awarded. However, he was granted a right to receive royalties on any future engines made and sold by the defendant to the design in question.

In Seager v Copydex Ltd:

Negotiations for a carpet grip foundered. Before this, the claimant had disclosed his design for a second grip and suggested a name - "Invisigrip." The defendants marketed a carpet grip later which they called "Invisigrip" and had a close resemblance to the plaintiff's design. **HELD:** Breach of confidence - unauthorised use of confidential information - too many coincidences and similarities.

Employees

Employers are entitled to protect genuine proprietary interests - where the employee has access to trade secrets or influence over clients. Restrictive covenants can be included in the contract of employment. However, there is a danger that attempts to restrict employees freedom of action (either during the lifetime of the contract or after its termination) will fall foul of the law on restraint of trade.

Employers cannot restrict general knowledge and skills acquired whilst working for them.

Even when trade secrets or trade connection are involved, the restraint must be reasonable both in terms of time and geographical area.

More recently, employers have started using long periods of notice (with a transfer to less significant work) or garden leave arrangements (a commitment to leave the employer and not work for another rival business for a defined period in exchange for full pay) as an alternative to restrictive covenants. They are subject to similar requirements of reasonableness by the courts.

Implied Duty of Fidelity

Even where the contract possesses no express restraint there is an implied duty to act faithfully and with the best interest of the employer in mind. This obligation is more demanding on existing employees (not for example, to work for rival businesses in their own time), than on ex-employees who continue to be subject to its coverage for a brief time afterwards. Again, passing on confidential information would involve a breach of this implied duty of fidelity. Employers will find using the implied duty more difficult when dealing with ex-employees after the case of *Faccenda Chicken Co. Ltd v Fowler* (1986) where the court seemed to restrict its operation significantly. Issues to be considered (when establishing whether a duty of confidentiality still exists) include :-

(1) the nature of the employment;

(2) the nature of the information;

(3) awareness of the employee re confidentiality of the material;

(4) the extent to which it is possible to separate secret information from non-secret material.

The facts of the case were as follows:

Faccenda Chicken Co. Ltd v Fowler

The employer's business consisted of supplying fresh chickens from itinerant refrigerated vans to retailers and caterers. The defendant was employed by the business as a sales manager. He left the company to set up business on his own account , taking eight of the plaintiff's employees with him. He started selling fresh chickens from refrigerated vans in the same area. A claim for breach of confidence was brought by his ex-employer, alleging that he was misusing confidential information which he had access to whilst employed by them. This consisted of sales information, including customers names and addresses, routes to customers, prices charged, and details of customers' usual orders. **HELD:** the information was within the scope of confidential information which could be covered by an express clause and would possibly be implied into the contract of an existing employee. However, it was not sufficiently important to allow an ex-employer to curtail its use by a former employee under a claim for breach of the implied duty of fidelity.

N.B. Consultants are generally subject to more demanding duties regarding confidential information, which will normally be covered by express provision. In the absence of express provision there is an implied duty in their contracts not to disclose, with a heavy presumption in favour of material being confidential.

Design Rights

The following section provides you with a description of the following aspects of the law on design rights:

- Classification of design rights – registered design, design right, design copyright
- Registered Design Right
- Definition
- Duration
- Requirements – novelty, industrial application, eye appeal
- Exclusions (including must match/must fit designs)
- Defences
- Remedies for infringement
- International registration
- Design Right (Unregistered)
- Comparison with registered design right
- Duration
- Definition
- Exclusions (including must match/must fit designs)
- Remedies

Legal protection of designs comes in three forms:

1 Registered designs (governed by the Registered Designs Act 1949 as amended)

2 Design right (dealing with unregistered designs, and regulated by the Copyright, Design and Patents Act 1988)

3 Copyright law, which overlaps with the above measures.

Designs can be for functional articles e.g. can opener, tool box, exhaust pipe. These will normally by governed by the design right (2 above)

Some designs may relate to decorative articles e.g. an attractive table lamp, a pattern for porcelain pottery. Such visually attractive designs are intended to appeal to the eye and are more appropriately covered by registered design protection (1 above)

In some cases, a design could be patentable (provided all the essentials are present). However, if any one is missing (e.g. lack of novelty), the above provisions would form the basis of intellectual property protection.

The registered design has much in common with a patent whereas the design right is more like a copyright.

Registered Design (Registered Designs Act 1949)

The most common kinds of designs which have been registered are for toys, games and electrical goods.

The distinguishing feature is that of eye appeal.

Whereas the design right applies mainly to functional designs, registered design applies to aesthetic articles.

Section 1(1) of the Registered Designs Act 1949 states that a design consists of "... features of shape, configuration, pattern or ornament applied to any article by an industrial process, being features which in the finished article appeal to and are judged by the eye."

The design must be 'new' (not previously registered or published in the UK prior to the date of application for registration). This does not mean that the design must be unlike any previous design. It does not have to exhibit 'novelty of a startling or groundbreaking variety to be valid'.

The design has to be applied to the article by 'an industrial process'. The law of registered design is aimed at industrial designs, being designs applied to manufactured articles which are mass produced. Regulations define industrial application as application to more than 50 articles.

The design must appeal to the eye of the prospective purchaser of the article, who is not deemed to be an expert in the field. It must have a material bearing on his decision to buy the product. In Lamson Industries

Ltd's Application, it was decided that a design for computer print-out paper having alternative coloured bands upon it was not registrable because the reason customers would buy the paper was that it would be easier to read, and because information could be printed out on the paper more closely spaced. Customers would buy the paper because of its utility and not because of its appearance.

Some designs may be disqualified for registration under s.1. These are:

- methods or principles of construction; or
- features of shape or configuration which are:
- dictated solely by the article's function, or
- dependent upon the appearance of another article or which the article is intended by the design's author to form an integral part.

These exclusions are justified in terms of preventing the right (effectively a monopoly) from becoming too strong and hindering the development of new designs for similar articles. Also, it enables free competition to operate for the manufacture of spare parts by other organisations (the must match exception

The importance of maintaining a free market in spare parts was stressed in *British Leyland Motor Corp. Ltd v Armstrong Patents Co. Ltd.* If a vehicle manufacturer was allowed to register the body panels of his cars he could charge exorbitant prices for replacement panels and refuse to grant licences to third party parts manufacturers or only in return for hefty royalties.

The must-match exception is fairly narrow and applies only if the design features are dependent on the appearance of another article and it is the author's intention that his articles form an integral part of the other article. It has been suggested that spare parts can be classified into two groups:

- Main body panels, doors, bonnet lids, windscreens (excluded)
- Wing mirrors, wheels, seats, steering wheels etc (not excluded)

It was argued that the latter can be made in a variety of designs to fit a particular vehicle as substitutions for the original parts while leaving the shape and general appearance of the vehicle unaffected.

Under rules passed in 1995, a number of further exclusions exist e.g. portraits of the royal family, flags of any country, insignia etc. without the consent of the appropriate authorities.

Registration gives its owner certain exclusive rights:

- to make or import for sale or hire or use for business purposes articles to which the design is attached

- to sell, hire etc. such articles

If anyone else does any of the above without a licence, it is an infringement.

Defences

There are a number of defences to an action for infringement, often based on attacking the validity of the registration e.g:

- The design was not new when registered

- The registration has expired

- (The 'Gillette' defence argues that either the alleged infringing design is not within the registered design or the registered design is invalid for lack of novelty.)

Registration

Applications are processed by the Designs Registry (a branch of the Patents Office). The current fee is £60 but other expenses are inevitable e.g. preparation of drawings or photographs. Many firms employ an agent for this work. The Registry carries out an examination and search. Simple applications could be dealt with in 3-4 months.

Duration

The initial registration period is 5 years but it can be renewed for a further four periods of 5 years (total of 25 years). Most designs have a limited commercial life, often 10-15 years maximum.

International Registration

If protection is required in another country, application must be made in each country involved. However, under the Paris Convention for Industrial Property 1883, a person who has applied for registration of a design in any of the Convention countries is given a priority with respect to applications to other Convention countries made within 6 months of the first application. Most of the industrialised counties in the world have ratified the Paris Convention.

Design Right

(Copyright, Designs and Patents Act 1988)

Until 1968 there was a gap in the protection of designs which were primarily functional. Copyright protected artistic works, patents covered new inventions and designs with eye appeal could be protected by registration. However, a design with none of the above features had no protection e.g. an overflow pipe for a washing machine. A number of changes were made, culminating in the creation of the design right – a right which automatically attaches to certain designs without the need for registration. It has been described as a weakened form of artistic copyright, which can be contrasted with the patent-like protection afforded registered designs. The duration of the design right is shorter, effectively no more than 10 years (and licences of right can be applied for in the last 5 years).

Examples of articles that can be protected include exhaust pipes (and other parts of motor vehicles), tools, kitchen equipment, office equipment and packaging.

Section 213(2) of the Copyright, Designs and Patents Act 1988 defines a design as 'the design of any aspect of the shape or configuration (whether internal or external) of the whole or part of an article.'

For the design right to apply to an article it must be original (not commonplace) and be in some tangible form e.g. recorded in a design document or by an article made to the design.

Exclusions exist which are similar to (but not identical with) those for registered design. The same justification applies i.e. preserving opportunities for development and a free market for spare parts. Surface decoration is also excluded because it is the natural preserve of registered design.

New and attractive designs can be the subject of the design right protection as well as registered design. However, an advantage of registration is that the period of protection is longer - a maximum of 25 years as against 15 years (or 10 from the product's first marketing). The form of protection is also stronger. Registering a design also provides proof that the owner is taking his legal rights seriously – something which can be made clear by attaching the fact of registration and the registration number on each article put on the market. It is also relatively inexpensive to register a design.

Because of the requirement for eye appeal, internal features relating to shape and configuration cannot be registered (although they receive protection under the design right).

Exclusions

The following are excluded from protection – Section 213(3):

- methods or principles of construction
- features or shape or configuration which:
- enable the article to be connected to, placed in, around or against another article so that either article may perform its function (the 'must-fit exception), or
- are dependent upon the appearance of another article of which the article is intended by the designer to form an integral part (the 'must match' exception)
- surface decoration

The must-fit and must-match exceptions have significant implications for the manufacturers of replacement parts (and to manufacturers of accessory parts e.g. a lamp to fit on a bicycle mounting or a dust-cover for a typewriter). Because of the must-fit exception, the features that must be a certain shape or configuration can be made without infringing the design right e.g. a television set and stand manufactured by a manufacturer. The connection between the two is not protected, but other design features of both the television and the stand are capable of protection.

An example of the must-match exception are replacement car doors. The external features must match the sweep of the bodywork. However, the inner skin (hidden from view by upholstery) is usually made of plastic. It often has holes for lightness and ribs for strength. The position of the holes and configuration of the ribs, if the design is original, could well be protected by the design right.

Design Copyright

Where a drawing forms the basis of a functional design it can be protected by copyright, provided it meets the requirements of originality and that a person who was not an expert could recognise the article as being reproduced from the drawing. The Copyright, Designs & Patents Act 1988 sought to rationalise the overlap between copyright and design rights:

- Where a work consists of or includes a design that is protected by copyright, the design right is suppressed in favour of the copyright (copying the drawing);

- Where the design is recorded in a drawing and a person makes an article using that drawing, he does not infringe copyright in the drawing although he does infringe design right (making the product);

- Where a person makes a photocopy of the drawing instead, copyright is infringed, but any subsequent making of articles from the copy will infringe design right only.

Copyright

This section will provide you with a description of the following features of copyright law:

- Background to the Copyright, Designs and Patents Act 1988 (CDPA)
- Duration of copyright
- Meaning of 'original' work
- Meaning & examples of literary work
- Exclusive rights gained through copyright
- Nature and classification of infringements (primary & secondary)
- Meaning of 'substantial part' of a work
- Exceptions to law of copyright (including 'fair dealing')

Objectives of the CDPA 1988

- To restate and amend earlier statute law on copyright (e.g. Copyright Act 1956)
- To take into account developments in new technology
- To rationalise design law where it overlapped with copyright
- To introduce the concept of moral rights for authors

New technology includes such everyday items as photocopiers, fax machines, e'mail, design tools and washing machines because all have computer programmes built into their composition.

Duration

Copyright lasts for the lifetime of the author, plus 70 years after the end of the calendar year in which the author dies (s.12).

The copyright of a work which an author enjoys is essentially of a negative character – the right to prevent other persons, individual or legal, from reproducing the work without permission. The work is deemed to possess economic value, being the result of time and effort. Competitors could gain an edge simply by copying the material and selling more cheaply.

There are, however, a number of important exceptions and qualifications which restrict the extent of an author's monopoly (see later).

An author will only enjoy rights in a literary work which is original. This relates to the source of the work. It does not mean that the work must be in substance original or possess inventive thought.

A literary work is defined in s.3 of the CDPA 1988 as any work, other than a dramatic or musical work, which is written, spoken, sung and, therefore includes

- a table or compilation, and

- a computer programme.

The definition includes:

- lists of customers, consignment notes, business letters, balance sheets actuarial tables, directories, tables of figures and football coupons. Drawings of engineering equipment may still be included, although, since 1988, these are more likely covered by design rights.

For a 'work' to be involved, some measure of skill and effort must have been invested in its creation. In one case, the copying of tables showing the values of leases and annuities was held not to be an infringement of copyright – the work could have been recalculated in a few hours and was relatively easy to have been reproduced.

Copyright cannot exist in a single word or title such as 'Hitachi' or 'Kojak'. *The case of Exxon v Exxon Insurance Ltd* is authority for this principle, where it was decided that, although Exxon was able to prove that it had gone to considerable time and trouble to decide on the name 'Exxon', it could not prevent copying through the law of copyright.

Under s.16, the author of a work enjoys exclusive rights to:

- Copy the work

- Issue copies of the work to the public

- Perform, show or play the work in public

- Broadcast the work or include it in a cable programme
- Make an adaptation of the work or do any of the above

Infringements are defined as the doing of any of the above acts in relation to the work either 'as a whole' or 'any substantial part of it' either directly or indirectly. Strict liability applies to the acts listed in s.16 and it is no defence to plead ignorance, or that one genuinely believed that there was an entitlement to copy. There are two types of infringement:

- Primary infringement – usually making the infringing copy
- Secondary infringement – dealing with the infringing copy

Copying the whole or a substantial part of a work can be an infringement. The question of what may be a substantial part of a protected work is one of fact in each case. Defining what is substantial is problematic though. A three-part test is employed:

- Has a qualifying work been copied?
- What is 'substantial' with reference to the quality of what has been taken?
- What is the value of what has been taken compared to the original?

The value of what has been copied has been addressed in a number of cases in terms of whether it identifies the earlier work or encapsulates it, and whether the labour and skill of an author has been unfairly appropriated. As a result, the courts will look beyond the volume of material reproduced and assess it in terms of the skill, labour and effort applied by the author.

Exceptions

Copyright is only a partial monopoly. There is no tort of copying and a number of important exceptions exist which permit a person to reproduce parts of the work of another. Some 50 sections of the 1988 Act provide a system of general rights to copy. The rationale for the permitted acts can be seen as a way of limiting the strength of the rights associated with copyright. It provides a fair balance between the rights of the copyright owner and the rights of society at large. Most of the permitted acts do not unduly interfere with the commercial exploitation of the work.

Two of the exceptions relate to *'fair dealing'*. Under s.29, it is fair dealing with a work to copy it for the purposes of private research and study. Section 30 permits the copying of a work for the purposes of criticism, review and reporting of current events.

The 1988 Act does not define 'fair dealing' and few cases have examined the concept. The courts have often held that taking a relatively small amount of a work is sufficient to be an infringement. They will look at a number of factors including the quantity and significance of the matter taken, whether the activity is in competition with the claimant, whether the work is published and whether the defendant acted maliciously.

Contractual Provision

IP rights can be strengthened by the drafting of suitable express contractual terms and conditions. Take the following example:

Infabrics Ltd, a private company with limited resources, has designed a new technical product which it wishes to develop. It has not registered any IP rights in the product. It decides to make a contract with A&G Manufacturing Ltd by which the latter agrees to manufacture the product on Infabrics behalf. Infabrics provide A&G with design drawings and technical specifications for this purpose. A&G will then produce all the specialist tools needed for manufacture.

Infabrics could, provided it has sufficient bargaining leverage over A&G, include the following terms which would enhance its position and reduce the risk of potential misuse of the confidential information made available to A&G:

- A confidentiality clause highlighting which information is regarded as confidential and stressing the limits to its legitimate use

- Clauses relating to ownership of tools, plans and designs relating to the product (which could include the right to insist on their return upon completion of the contract – the value of the tools manufactured by A&G being taken into account in the initial pricing agreement)

- A clause concerning ownership of the finished products, including defective ones which fail quality control checks
- A clause permitting periodical inspection of the production site to ensure compliance with the above contractual arrangements

The presence of a general IP rights clause would certainly increase the awareness of A&G of its IP obligations and the fact that Infabrics are taking its rights seriously.

The above situation could well be covered by an implied duty to use confidential information only for authorised purposes even in the absence of *express contractual provision. In Saltman Engineering v Campbell*:

Confidential designs for new tools were given to the defendants so they could manufacture the tools exclusively for the plaintiffs. The defendants started to manufacture and sell them on their own account. **HELD**: Breach of confidence.

Contract provisions relating to IPR need to cover three issues:

- Definition
- Ownership
- Protection

Definition provisions will identify clearly the type(s) of IPR covered by the agreement. They may refer to know-how and define knowhow in terms of patents, design rights, copyright, guidance manuals etc.

Issues of ownership of IPR in a contract become more complicated where new IPR is to developed during the life-span of the contract. This involves background and foreground IPR. . Pre-existing rights are known as background IPR – rights which each party already possesses and which it will be contributing to the successful performance of the contract. Intellectual property rights which are created during the course of the contract are called foreground IPR.

The contract will usually go on to specify types of licence that will permit future use of the product in question eg. software.

Protection is achieved through the inclusion of warranties. These need to cover both fitness for purpose (that the software, patented invention etc. does the job it is supposed to do) and potential third party claims. The latter relates to possible claims by the holders of existing IP rights that the purchaser is infringing these rights i.e. that the seller had no right to supply the product without the appropriate permission.Suitable indemnities should be included in the contract to obtain protection against such possibilities.

In conclusion:

- Intellectual Property Rights (IPR) are based on either protection of creative effort or commercial reputation

- It can be classified into either hard IPR (requiring registration) or soft IPR (granted automatically)

- Remedies for infringement are injunctions, damages, account of profits and seizure of infringing goods

- The relevant forms of IPR are patents, trade marks, passing off, breach of confidence, design rights and copyright

- Attempts to modernise the law on IPR has resulted in the Patents Act 1977, the Copyright, Patents and Designs Act 1988, the Trade Marks Act 1994 and a range of EU Directives covering most of the above forms of IPR

- There still exists important common law protection – the actions for breach of confidence and passing off

- Contractual provisions can strengthen the rights of a party by explicitly defining issues relating to coverage, ownership and protection against infringement of IPR

Chapter 17
International Trade

The long distances involved in international sale of goods means that the parties usually have little opportunity to engage in active or detailed negotiation. There is consequently a need to rely on standard documentation containing well-established trade terms with which both parties are familiar. The following set of notes outlines the main documentation involved.

Documentation for Import and Export

Up to 4 separate contracts can be involved in buying goods from abroad:-

■ the actual purchase contract

■ a contract of carriage

■ a contract of insurance

■ a contract of finance (often involving a letter of credit - see later)

Each involves costs and the parties need to decide how they are to be allocated. This is done by choosing from a range of standard contractual provisions known as Incoterms. Over many years a number of trade terms were developed to deal with the special conditions of international trade. They were subsequently codified by the International Chamber of Commerce (ICC) and now provide a widely accepted uniform system. Incoterms consists of agreed explanations of many of the terms used in international trade and defines the duties of the seller and buyer. The 2000 edition covers 13 such terms including ex works, FOB and CIF.

Incoterms must be expressly incorporated into the contract if they are to apply. There is no automatic incorporation by operation of law. The parties will need to agree on which one of the 13 possible Incoterms is the most appropriate for their particular contract.

The benefit of using Incoterms is to minimise the risk of ambiguity and misunderstanding between the parties. Amongst other things, the choice of which terms to use will affect who is responsible for making the arrangements for carriage, who bears the cost and who bears the risk of accidental damage.

Commonly used Expressions

CIF Contracts

The initials stand for cost, insurance and freight as these stand for the three main items of expenditure incurred by the seller in shipment of the goods. Therefore, if A purchases goods from B on CIF terms, the price quoted by B will include all necessary expenditure involved in the shipment of those goods, i.e. the price of the goods themselves, the premium for insuring them in transit and the freight costs for their carriage by ship to their port of destination.

It should be noted that the terminology used by the parties should not be treated as conclusive. It is feasible for the parties to nominate a contract cif, but on examination of all the circumstances, for it to become apparent that this description is inaccurate.

Property in the goods (ownership) normally passes when the documents are handed over to the buyer. CIF contracts are sometimes described as 'document driven' transactions. If the seller has handed over the correct shipping documents, he is entitled to be paid, irrespective of where the goods are at the time, or their condition.

In other words, the seller performs the contract by delivery up of the shipping documents (effectively the bill of lading) – not the delivery of the goods. The buyer cannot defer payment until after inspection of the goods. However, this in no way prejudices the buyer's right to reject the goods as defective once they do arrive.

The seller's main duties can best be summarised as follows:-

- make out an invoice of goods sold

- ship at the port of shipment goods answering the description in the contract

- procure a contract for freighting the goods by ship to the destination referred to in the contract

- arrange for insurance of the goods during shipment

- within a reasonable time send to the buyer the shipping documents concerned (i.e. invoice, bill of lading, policy of insurance etc.)

In addition, he will be required to obtain export clearance. However, the buyer will be expected to bear the cost of unloading and import duties.

FOB Contracts (or strict fob)

The initials stand for free on board. The seller places the contract goods on the agreed vessel at the agreed port of shipment and all the costs of carriage are borne by the buyer. It is therefore not the seller who is the shipper, but the buyer, who receives the bill of lading directly through his agent.

This will obviously affect the passing of property and risk. Normally property in the goods passes to the buyer the moment the goods go on board. It is important to note, however that there are exceptions to this rule which are quite significant. For example, if the goods are loaded as part of a larger consignment of goods of the same description, so that at point of loading they are unascertained, then property will only pass when there is an unconditional appropriation of suitable goods in a deliverable state.

Since risk usually passes with ownership, any damage occurring prior to shipment is the seller's responsibility. Once the goods are over the ship's rail the buyer assumes responsibility for any damage.

The buyer is required to nominate an effective ship (one which is ready, willing and able to carry the goods in question) and this should be notified in reasonable time to the seller. If the nominated ship proves unsuitable, the buyer can re-nominate another ship provided this leaves the seller with enough time to carry out his responsibilities.

The seller is required to nominate a shipping date and notify the buyer of that date.

Note that some contracts are designated "fob - additional services". Under such contracts, the parties may re-allocate their obligations. In particular certain duties, normally those of the buyer, may be undertaken by the seller as the buyer's agent. It does not normally, however, make any difference to the passing of property in the goods.

Usually the fob seller's duties may be summarised as follows:

- make an invoice of the goods sold
- to ship at the port of shipment, goods of the description in the contract
- to nominate a shipping date and notify the buyer of that date
- to tender to the buyer the invoice and the bill of lading

The seller is responsible for all expenses and costs incurred in getting the goods over the ship's rail e.g. if the ship is delayed, he will have to bear the additional storage costs.

Where the contract is fob - additional services, and the seller acts as agent for the buyer, he will often undertake duties such as procuring appropriate insurance - but of course this will be at the buyer's expense.

Free Alongside Ship

The seller performs his duties when the goods have been placed alongside the ship on the quay (or in lighters) at the port of shipment named by the buyer on the correct date or within the agreed period. Since 2000, the seller is required to obtain the necessary export licence. The buyer then assumes responsibility for all costs and risks from that point.

Ex Works (EXW)

The seller fulfils his duties when he has made the goods available at his premises. He is not obliged to load them on the lorry provided by the buyer or for arranging export clearance (unless otherwise agreed). The buyer incurs all the costs and risks connected with the transit. This is the minimum commitment from the seller's point of view and should be reflected in a lower price for the contract. Specifically, the seller is required to:

- Supply goods in conformity with the contract of sale
- Place the goods at the disposal of the buyer at the point of delivery named by the buyer
- Package the goods suitably to allow for their collection
- Give reasonable notification to the buyer of when the goods are available
- Bear the risk and costs connected with the goods until collection.

The buyer, in turn, is required to:

- Take delivery of the goods as soon as they are placed at his disposal
- Make arrangements for the carriage of the goods from the seller's premises
- Bear all risks and costs from the time they have been placed at his disposal, including the costs of any export/import documentation

DDP (Delivery Duty Paid)

DDP contracts are the most favourable from the buyer's viewpoint. It means that the seller bears all costs, expenses and risks in getting the goods to the place specified by the seller, usually his place of business in the country of importation. This involves obtaining the necessary export and import licences, and paying port taxes, export duties, and miscellaneous other charges.

- Carriage to be arranged by the seller
- Risk transfer from the seller to the buyer when the goods are placed at the disposal of the buyer
- Costs transfer from the seller to the buyer when the goods are placed at the disposal of the buyer

Bills of Lading

"a document signed by the shipowner or by the master or other agent on behalf of the shipowner, which states that certain goods have been shipped on a particular ship or have been received for shipment." (Charlesworth's Business Law - Sweet & Maxwell)

- It sets out the terms on which goods have been delivered to and received by the shipowner
- Once signed by/on behalf of the carrier, it is handed to the shipper (usually the owner; usually the exporter)

The law relating to bills of lading is contained in both common law and legislation, especially the Carriage of Goods by Sea Act 1992.

Characteristics

Document of Title

This amounts to conclusive proof of ownership. Upon receipt of the bill of lading, the carrier must transfer the goods to the importer as owner. Bearer bills (made out to 'consignee', or 'to shipper's order' or 'bearer') can be transferred to another person by assignment which enables the purchase/sale of goods whilst in transit. The assignee can claim the goods by presenting the bill on the vessel's arrival at the port of destination. Transfer of a bill of lading amounts to a symbolic delivery of the goods (a constructive transfer of possession).

Receipt

The bill is issued by or on behalf of the carrier to acknowledge receipt of the goods. It provides evidence of the identity, quantity and condition of goods, and usually includes details of identification marks. This enables the buyer to identify defects acquired in transit which become the responsibility of the carrier. It will contain a statement on the condition of the goods at time of shipment. If the bill of lading says the goods are in apparent good order then this is a "clean" bill; if the carrier has any reservations then the bill will be "claused" or "dirty".

Evidence of Terms

The bill also provides proof of the terms of the contract of carriage - the contract between the shipper and the carrier. This can be either a charterparty ("a contract whereby the charterer hires the use of a ship from the shipowner.") or a contract of carriage on a general ship where an entire ship is not needed.

A bill of lading may be of several different types. It may be in complete form, containing all the clauses, or an abbreviated version - a 'short form bill' - containing only the more important clauses.

It may be a 'containerised bill' where the shipped goods are packed in containers or a 'combined transport bill' where the shipment requires not only carriage of the goods on board ship, but other modes of transport as well. "Received for shipment" bills indicate that the goods have been received by the carrier and held under his control whereas a "shipped" bill indicates that the goods have actually been placed on board ship.

Contracts of Carriage of Goods

Charterparties

These are contracts involving the hire of an entire ship (either for a defined period of time, or for a particular voyage). The document sets out the duties of the shipowner and the rights and duties of the hirer. It will identify the vessel, indicate its carrying capacity and tonnage, specify its availability, state the hire fee and the period of hire. Most charterparties will be arranged on the basis that the master and crew remain the servants of the shipowner (technically described as a charterparty not by way of demise). The division of responsibility between shipowner and charterer has been described as follows:

"The charterer might direct where the vessel is to go and with what she is to be laden but the shipowner remains in all respects accountable for the manner in which she may be navigated."

Demurrage & Lay Days

The charterparty will normally specify a set number of days when the vessel will be engaged in loading and unloading cargo – the lay days. If this number is exceeded, the charterer will usually be required to pay compensation for the delay caused. The amount will be set out in the charterparty and is known as 'demurrage'. It is a form of liquidated damages and must satisfy the rules relating to penalties.

Contract of Carriage on a general ship

When an entire ship in not needed, a contract of carriage on a general ship will be arranged. Once the goods have been placed on board the vessel, the shipowner will issue the shipper with a bill of lading to cover his goods and no others. Such contracts need to strike a balance between the interests of the carrier and the interests of the shipper on such matters as risk of loss or damage to the goods. Various international conventions have been negotiated to specify the obligations of the carrier and at present two such conventions operate across the world. A protocol was agreed in Brussels in 1968 which created the Hague-Visby Rules, the latter being incorporated into English law by the Carriage of Goods by Sea Act 1971. Some countries felt that the Hague-Visby Rules favoured the carrier too much and another set of rules were formulated in 1978 known as the Hamburg Rules. Today, both sets of rules exist with some countries favouring one and other countries preferring the alternative:

Hague-Visby Rules	Hamburg Rules
UK	US
France	Germany
Netherlands	Spain
Sweden	Australia
Belgium	and others
& others	

We shall focus on the Hague-Visby Rules for obvious reasons. These imply a set of duties which are imposed on the carrier. The Rules do not automatically attach to contracts of carriage involving UK companies, but will apply in the vast majority of cases e.g. any voyage where the port of shipment is in the UK, voyages where the port of shipment is in a country which is a signatory to the Hague-Visby Rules, voyages where the contract refers explicitly to the Hague-Visby Rules.

There are three main duties imposed on the carrier:

- To provide a seaworthy ship
- To properly load, stow, carry and discharge the goods
- To issue a bill of lading on the demand of the shipper

To provide a seaworthy ship

This is not an absolute duty. The carrier is required to exercise due diligence to provide a seaworthy ship. This includes issues such as the design, structure and condition of the vessel and equipment, the competency and sufficiency of the crew, and the manner in which the cargo is stowed

2   To properly load, stow, carry and discharge the goods

These tasks must be properly carried out i.e. a recognised system must be used and one which is suitable to the particular requirements of the cargo involved e.g. cargoes which may taint each other should not be stowed near each other. The standard of care required is one of reasonableness. This duty, with regard to loading of goods, is subject to significant exclusions available to the carrier. If goods are damaged or destroyed owing to fire (unless caused by the carrier), perils, dangers and accidents of the sea, Acts of God, strikes & other industrial stoppages and various other events, the carrier will not be liable.

Liability for loss or damage is limited to a maximum level, details of which are set out within the Hague-Visby Rules.

3   To issue a bill of lading on the demand of the shipper

The carrier is obliged, after receiving the goods, to issue a bill of lading containing specified details (e.g. loading marks necessary for identification of the goods, number of packages or pieces, apparent order and condition of the goods) on the demand of the shipper

Payment Methods and Instruments

Additional complications where international trade involved:-

- distances
- risks of international transportation
- limited direct contact
- different legal systems

All affect the seller's confidence in receiving payment. Some form of greater security is required and this is achieved through the use of banks as intermediaries. Although collection agreements are possible whereby the seller will obtain payment from a bank in the buyer's country, documentary credits have been the most popular method of payment in international contracts – "the lifeblood of commerce" according to more than one judge. The most common form of documentary credit is the letter of credit.

Letters of Credit

This in an undertaking by a bank to a seller, made on behalf of a purchaser, that payment will be made on presentation of the appropriate documents. Once the seller delivers the documents of title (e.g. an invoice, a bill of lading and an insurance certificate) to a bank is his own country, payment will be made. The bank in the seller's country remits the documents to the buyer's bank in his country, which passes them on to the buyer in exchange for the sum paid (+ commission).

Seller   **Advising bank**   **Issuing Bank**   **Buyer**

Buyer instructs bank in his own country (issuing bank) to open a credit with bank in seller's country (advising bank) in favour of the seller.

Seller will be able to draw on this credit (i.e. obtain funds from advising bank) upon delivery to the advising bank of any documents specified by the buyer (e.g. clean bill of lading)

Advising bank hands over the documents to issuing bank and is reimbursed for sum advanced.

Issuing bank presents the documents to the buyer in return for payment

Benefits

Using this technique, risks (of non-delivery or non-payment) are minimised. The bank will not pay the seller unless the appropriate documents of title are produced. The seller, in return, has the assurance that payment will be made before the buyer assumes control of the goods. Additionally, payment will be in his own country.

Disadvantage

Delay because multiple parties are involved e.g. goods can arrive at the port of destination before the buyer has received the bill of lading from the issuing bank.

Types of Letters of Credit

Revocable & Unconfirmed

There is no commitment on the part of either the issuing bank or the advising bank. This offers little protection to the seller that the money will be paid. The buyer will be able to terminate the arrangement at any time.

Irrevocable & Unconfirmed

The issuing bank is bound to honour the credit even if the buyer has attempted to revoke the payment. However, if the issuing bank refuses, it will be necessary to pursue a complaint in the country where the bank is located.

Irrevocable and Confirmed

Both banks are committed to honouring the payment. If either refuses, the seller can pursue an action against the advising bank in his own country.

Even where fraud is involved, e.g. the shipment itself is fraudulent or the documents are forged, there must be clear evidence before the banks can refuse payment.

Banks insist on strict compliance in relation to the documents to be handed over and will refuse to make the payment where even minor discrepancies are involved.

The Shipping Documents

Commercial invoice

The invoice is a claim by the exporter for payment from the importer under the terms of the sales contract. It should include a description of the goods, together with unit prices, if appropriate, amount payable, shipping marks and shipping terms. All these details must also match exactly the information stipulated in the letter of credit. Normally several copies of the invoice are required by the customs authorities overseas. The invoice should also state the price of the goods as agreed by both importer and exporter, using the standard price terms (Incoterms).

Bill of lading

This document is the receipt given to the exporter by the shipping company for goods accepted for transport by sea. It conveys title to the goods when in negotiable form. The bill of lading names the shipper and the consignee (importer) or the consignee's agent and it is signed on behalf of the carrier. If it is issued to order, it is transferable by the party named as shipper or, if issued to the order of a named party, it is transferable by that party, in both cases by endorsement.

Bills of lading are normally issued in sets of two, three or more originals, any one of which may be used to obtain delivery of the goods. The number of originals in a set is shown on each document. As soon as one original is presented to the carrier at the port of destination in order to obtain release of the goods, the carrier's liability is discharged even if the true owner were to present another original. For complete control over the goods, therefore, it is necessary to possess a full set. Non-negotiable copies, which are unsigned, are not documents of title and are used only for record purposes. Most letters of credit call for full sets to be presented to the bank before the exporter is paid.

Insurance policy or certificate

Proof that the goods are covered for risk of damage or loss during transit is often asked for in the letter of credit, which will call for either an insurance policy or an insurance certificate. (However, certificates issued by insurance brokers are not acceptable unless specifically permitted by the credit).

Regular exporters can arrange to cover all exports over a particular period, thereby avoiding the need to take out a fresh policy with each shipment. In this case individual insurance certificates are issued for each shipment - either by the insurers or by the exporter.

Certificate of origin

Most countries require a certificate that shows evidence of the country of origin of the goods being imported. Letters of credit often stipulate the presentation of this document, which may be issued by the exporter himself or by a Chamber of Commerce or Consular authority, as specified.

Bills of exchange

A bill of exchange is legally defined as 'an unconditional order in writing, addressed by one person to another, signed by the person giving it, requiring the person to whom it is addressed to pay on demand or at a fixed or determinable future time a sum certain in money to, or to the order of, a specified person or to bearer'.

In the case of a letter of credit transaction, it is drawn up by the exporter (the drawer) and is an order to the importer or the paying bank (the drawee) to pay a specified amount of money immediately (a sight bill) or at a future date (a usance bill). In the case of a usance bill, the drawee acknowledges and accepts liability for the exporter's claim for payment by signing an acceptance across it. The wording on the bill of exchange must match exactly the terms of the credit.

A single bill of exchange (called a sola bill) may be presented, provided that the credit does not stipulate that bills are required in duplicate.

In conclusion:

- International trade involves the use of a number of specialised documents and terms and conditions that are recognised throughout the commercial world

- These include bills of lading, charterparties, the Hague-Visby Rules, Incoterms and letters of credit

- Bills of lading fulfil a number of functions, namely, constituting a document of title to the goods, proof of receipt of the goods by the shipping company and evidence of the terms of the contract of carriage – the charterparty

- The charterparty, if subject to English law, will often include the Hague-Visby Rules which impose a number of duties on the shipper and the carrier

- The charterparty will usually include the definitions contained in Incoterms relating to relevant obligations such as CIF, FOB, FAS etc, thus reducing ambiguity or misunderstanding between the parties

- Letters of credit (or documentary credits) are frequently used to facilitate payment in international transactions

Chapter 18
International Sale of Goods

There have been several attempts to harmonise or align contractual regulation of contracts involving businesses from different countries. At present, the UK has ratified the Hague Convention and implemented its provisions in 1967.

This short chapter identifies the main provisions of the Hague Convention as implemented through the Uniform Laws on International Sales Act 1967 and the approach adopted by the Rome Convention on the Laws Applicable to Contractual Obligations.

There are a number of international conventions that attempt to achieve a greater degree of uniformity of rights and obligations where companies from different countries enter into sale of goods contracts with each other.

The Uniform Laws on International Sales Act 1967 was passed to give effect to two Conventions signed at a conference at The Hague in 1964. The two Conventions are incorporated in the Act as schedules:

- Schedule 1 The Uniform Law on the International Sale of Goods
- Schedule 2 The Uniform Law on the Formation of Contracts for the International Sale of Goods

The Act is part of the English law and, whenever English law governs a contract, the provisions of Schedule 1 apply if the parties expressly state that this is their wish. The benefit is that a set of terms that are well-recognised in different countries will then decide rights and duties between the parties.

Schedule 1 contains provisions governing the seller's obligations as to:

- the time and place of delivery
- the insurance and carriage of the goods
- the conformity of the goods with the contract
- the giving of good title

Other provisions relate to:

- the passing of risk
- the buyer's obligations as to payment and taking delivery

There are some significant differences with English contract law. The Uniform Laws do not recognise the concept of 'condition,' breach of which entitles the buyer to reject the goods. An alternative concept is used – that of 'fundamental breach.' The consequences of the breach would have to be assessed in order to establish whether the buyer has a right to reject

Schedule 2 applies to the formation of contracts and its provisions are concerned with the rules of offer and acceptance:

- An offer is generally revocable until the offeree has despatched his acceptance
- An offer is not revocable if it either states a fixed time for acceptance or else indicates that it is irrevocable
- A qualified acceptance will normally be construed as a rejection of the offer and a counter offer.

(However), if the qualification consists of additional or different terms which do not materially alter the terms of the offer, it will constitutes a binding acceptance unless the offeror promptly objects to the discrepancy.

A late acceptance may be treated by the buyer as having arrived in time, provided the offeror promptly informs the acceptor that he regards it as binding.

A late acceptance which suffers from unusual delay in transit and which would in normal transit have arrived in time is regarded as being in time unless the offeror promptly informs the acceptor that he considers his offer lapsed.

The UN Convention on Contracts for the International Sale of Goods ('Vienna Convention')

The Vienna Convention is a further development of the attempt to unify the law here. It is founded on the two Hague Conventions of 1964 and is intended to supersede them. The Vienna Convention combines the topics treated in the two Hague Conventions into one document.

However, although many countries have now ratified it, the UK has not as yet given effect to the Convention. The earlier Conventions continue to apply in the meantime.

International Contracts – Which law governs the contract?

Problems can arise over which law applies to a contract where the two parties operate from different countries. The position is now governed by the Contracts (Applicable Law) Act 1990 which adopted the Rome Convention on the Law Applicable to Contractual Obligations 1980 – again a measure intended to harmonise the position across all member states.

Essentially, it is for the parties to choose which law applies to the contract. This can be achieved expressly in the contract (either by specific provision stating which law applies, or by reasonable deduction from the terms of the contract) or established from the circumstances of the contract e.g. the previous course of dealing between the two parties.

If the above approach cannot decide the issue, it is a matter of deciding which law is most closely connected to the contract. There is a presumption in favour of the performer's habitual residence being the most closely connected e.g. the seller in a contract for sale of goods. 'Habitual residence' means generally the place of business of the party performing the contract. This presumption can be rebutted if the law of another country would be more closely connected to the country e.g. the country in which a construction contract is taking place.

In conclusion:

- The Hague Convention 1964 was an attempt to harmonise the laws governing international contracts

- Its main provisions on contract and formation of contract were ratified in the UK by the passing of the Uniform Laws on International Sales Act 1967

- There is significant commonality between these provisions and UK law of contract but there are also differences

- The Vienna Convention 1980 was an attempt to improve on the earlier document, but has not yet been ratified by the UK

- The law governing a contract is regulated by the Contracts (Applicable Law) Act 1990, adopting the Rome Convention 1980

Chapter 19
Dispute Resolution

The traditional approach to disputes has been to avoid litigation by using arbitration where negotiation has failed to achieve settlement. There were strong arguments for this preference in earlier years but these had become weaker for a number of reasons. Some reform of arbitration procedures was carried out in 1996 to address the problem. There has still been a growing trend towards the use of mediation in recent years, combined with an increase in another alternative – adjudication.

The chapter contains an explanation of the following legal issues:

- Classification of alternative dispute resolution procedures
- Identification of main concerns/requirements of parties involved
- Comparison of mediation and conciliation
- Comparison of adjudication and arbitration
- Reform of arbitration – the Arbitration Act 1996
- Litigation

There are a number of alternative methods to deal with conflicts:

- By agreement
- By intervention
- By third party determination
- Through litigation

What do organisations want from a dispute resolution procedure?

Recent research suggests the following preferences (in descending order):

- Speed
- Commercial pragmatism
- Fairness and equity
- Low cost
- Confidentiality
- Protection of business relationships

Speed is by far and away the most important issue (which would explain the preference for arbitration over litigation and partly the increasing use of adjudication over arbitration). It would clearly seem that speed and cost are the essential ingredients desired by organisations wishing to resolve a conflict. Whether these specific objectives are critical to the organisation will depend on the situation involved. Future trading relations, the protection of its public reputation, the need to be seen to be enforcing its rights (for future deterrent purposes) also can play an important role in business objectives.

Resolution by Intervention

These methods occupy an intermediate position between negotiation and third party determination. Their more recent title is alternative dispute resolution (ADR). They consist of two basic approaches:

- Mediation
- Conciliation

Both involve a third party being brought in to facilitate discussion and resolution. It is sometimes called assisted negotiation.

What is the difference between mediation and conciliation?

The mediator merely facilitates discussion whereas the conciliator provides the parties with a recommendation based on his opinions.

In 1990, the CBI created the Centre for Dispute Resolution (CEDR) to encourage mediation (and other methods of dispute handling).

The mediation process is somewhat like shuttle diplomacy – the parties meet in joint and separate meetings, the mediator moving between them, attempting to find points of common ground and build on them. It has to be treated as an entirely voluntary exercise, and either side can withdraw at any stage. It does not require pre-agreed contractual terms for it to be adopted but if such a provision has been drafted into the contract (e.g. an alternative dispute resolution clause) it can oblige the parties to use the process, even though one of both have changed their minds. However, there is some doubt on this point, as it would seem improbable that the courts would enforce a non-binding negotiation method on the parties.

Although a settlement is initially not legally binding on the parties it is usual for it to be documented and signed as a contractually enforceable agreement.

There is considerable similarity between mediation and conciliation. Conciliation is entirely voluntary and is undertaken on a confidential basis. The parties prepare statements of their view on the disputed issue to send to the conciliator. He commences an investigation by interviewing the parties. Unlike an arbitrator he does not have to observe the principles of natural justice (see later). He adopts an inquisitorial method, controlling the collection of evidence and questioning the parties involved. A meeting is then arranged at which the conciliator begins to form an opinion (possibly with an 'expert' present to assist and advise on technical issues). He will express his views on the strengths and weaknesses of the parties' cases and offer an opinion of how an arbitrator may view the dispute. This is partly being done to encourage a possible settlement between the parties. Failing this, the conciliator will issue his own recommendation. The following points can be made about this recommendation:

- It is only the opinion of the conciliator
- It is not justified with reasons (unless specifically requested)
- It is not binding ('without prejudice')
- It is a practical solution, not necessarily in strict accord with the relevant law)

The process may take about 3 months to complete.

Advantages of Mediation/Conciliation

- Speed (for mediation just a few days; for conciliation not exceeding 2 3 months)
- Inexpensive (sometimes less than 1% of disputed amount)
- Confidential
- Non-binding
- Parties able to agree settlement
- Flexible outcomes (commercial trade-offs etc)
- Encourages future trade relations with other party

Third Party Determination

This part of the spectrum of conflict resolution methods contains the following approaches:

- Adjudication
- Arbitration
- Litigation

All involve a third party presiding on the issues and pronouncing a judgement of his own i.e. the parties lose control on the outcome.

Adjudication and arbitration have much in common - the parties agree who shall play the judicial role, present their cases and receive a judgement. However, there are significant differences in approach. Nevertheless, there remains widespread confusion in business as to their respective meanings. In fact the terminology used in the contract is not conclusive as to which process would apply in the event of a dispute. For example, the contract may specify that 'adjudication' would operate. If it then proceeded to describe procedures which were essentially arbitral, the courts would insist on arbitration being used.

Arbitration is a process by which it is agreed by the parties that an independent third party is brought in to make a decision which is binding on the parties. The power (jurisdiction) of the arbitrator will be derived either from the consent of the parties or from a court order or from statute clearly indicating use of arbitration. The choice of arbitrator will be for the parties to decide, or according to a method to which they have consented. He must act impartially and fairly, applying the principles of natural justice to the proceedings.

Bearing these points in mind, some clear differences can be identified from adjudication. The adjudicator makes a decision which is non-binding (unless specifically agreed otherwise). He examines the evidence and makes appropriate enquiries, Being an expert, he uses his own skill and judgement in order to formulate a decision. An arbitrator, conversely, makes an award which is final and binding, after receiving presentations from both parties according to the principles of natural justice. The latter process is therefore more thorough and time-consuming.

Why has adjudication emerged in recent years?

It was a reaction to some of the growing failings of arbitration. Originally, arbitration was established to provide a more informal, quicker and cheaper method of resolving disputes to the courts. By the early 1990's opinion viewed it as increasingly formal, slow and expensive, partly as a result of increased lawyer involvement ('wigless litigation'). Among other criticisms it was argued that procedure imitated High Court actions which made hearings as lengthy as litigation and could cost even more. It was also relatively easy to appeal against the decision of the arbitrator and the subsequent appeal case could take years to reach a decision.

It was argued that, although there were some occasions where disputes are so important and/or complex to justify elaborate arbitration proceedings, there were many others which did not require such thoroughness. What was more important was a speedy resolution to the dispute, even if it was achieved at the expense of detailed scrutiny. Adjudication provided this alternative, albeit more superficial, approach.

Something had to be done to improve the arbitration process in the face of all these mounting criticisms.

Reform of Arbitration

Parliament passed the Arbitration Act 1996 in an effort to make arbitration more attractive. The Act intended to improve the position in the following ways:

- It redrafted and codified the law on arbitration in clearer language.
- It placed the arbitrator in firm control of the proceedings
- It placed a duty on the arbitrator to operate cost-effective methods, depending on the size and complexity of the dispute
- It reduced the ability of appeals to the court

This has improved the attractiveness of arbitration in comparison with litigation in the courts. However, it has to be remembered that the civil court system has also been significantly reformed in the last few years. The cost and time involved in many civil actions will now often be less off-putting since the recommendations of the Woolf Report have been implemented (see section on Litigation).

The Arbitration Act 1996 made a significant number of other improvements:

Procedures

Arbitration no longer has to follow High Court procedures closely. It is no longer possible to appeal simply because court procedures were not carefully observed. Appeals will only be possible for serious procedural irregularities

Linked to the above, arbitrators are expected to adopt procedures which are suitable to the particular case before them. The only underlying requirement is that they give both parties a reasonable opportunity to put their case

Linked to this, arbitration should become shorter and cheaper in many disputes.

Powers of Arbitrator

The arbitrator now has the right to decide all procedural issues, subject to agreement by both parties. This has simplified and clarified the previous position.

Court Intervention

The courts now hold a predominantly supportive role in connection with arbitration

Courts can assist by making orders for the attendance of witnesses, to enforce orders and to appoint a new arbitrator if one resigns or dies

Courts, in certain situations, can grant an interim injunction in support of an arbitration.

Removal of an Arbitrator

The courts can only act to remove an arbitrator if:

- Any available recourse to a relevant arbitral body has been exhausted, and one of the following is involved:
- there are justifiable doubts as to the impartiality of the arbitrator
- he is incapable of conducting the proceedings
- he has failed to conduct the proceedings properly or reasonable quickly, and by doing so, has caused substantial injustice

Appeals

1 Appeal on the Merits

- The arbitration agreement may exclude any right to challenge the decision on its merits

- If it does not, appeal must have the consent of all the parties or leave of the court

- The court will only give its consent if the award is obviously wrong, or, where the question is one of general public importance, is open to serious doubt

2 Appeal on Procedural Grounds

There must be a serious irregularity, which includes failure to give reasons (unless agreed beforehand) and ambiguity in the detail of the award.

Costs

This can be agreed between the parties themselves (but only after the dispute has arisen). Otherwise, the arbitrator will decide on the allocation of costs. This will normally be on the general principle that the winner will have his reasonable costs paid for by the loser. The arbitrator may assess the costs to be awarded, or, failing this, the court will decide the matter. The general rule is that the winner will be able to recover a reasonable amount for costs reasonable incurred.

Arbitration Fees

The fees involved, including the hire of suitable facilities, will frequently far exceed those paid to the court in litigation.

Litigation

Advantages of Litigation

- Thorough
- Full access to natural justice
- Full legal representation
- Decisive, final and binding
- Ideal if dispute is over a point of law

International Arbitration

Some special features only operate where international arbitration is involved. Clearly some of the earlier advantages still apply:

- Cost
- Speed
- Confidentiality
- Expertise
- Influence over selection of arbitrator

Some other benefits of international arbitration include:

- Control over where (which country) it takes place
- Control over which law governs the proceedings

Additional disadvantages include:

Potential legal complexity

In theory, three different legal systems can be relevant in international arbitration. The disputed contract could be governed by the laws of one country; the arbitration procedures could be governed by the laws of another; the interpretation of the arbitration agreement itself (e.g. its scope) could be governed by another. It is obvious that considerable confusion can be caused in such situations. In practice, it is normal for the law governing the disputed contract also to be the law governing interpretation of the arbitration agreement and for the law governing procedure to be that of the country where the hearing is being held.

Enforcement of the Award

Clearly there can be problems attached to enforcing arbitration awards where the other party is situated in another part of the world. To assist enforcement, the succinctly named New York Convention on the Recognition & Enforcement of Foreign Arbitral Awards 1958 (between friends - the New York Convention) was agreed. Convention awards are enforced in the same manner as an English award where the agreement was made in a country which has acceded to the Convention. Over 80 countries have already done so.

Complications of Appeal to the Courts in another country

The usual procedure is for such appeals to go to the courts in the country where the arbitration hearing took place. Thus, the case could be decided according to a legal system which had nothing to do with the parties who agreed the contract.

Language problems and obtaining suitable legal assistance

In conclusion:

- In dispute resolution, the main requirements of the parties are speed, the adoption of a pragmatic approach, fairness, low cost, confidentiality and the protection of business relationships
- Dispute resolution methods include third party intervention and third party determination (other than courts)
- These are sometimes referred to as Alternative Dispute Resolution (ADR)
- Third party intervention comprises mediation and conciliation
- Third party determination comprises adjudication and arbitration

- Arbitration procedures have been extensively amended by the Arbitration Act 1996 in the light of heavy criticism

- The popularity of arbitration (over litigation) has been waning in recent years, with mediation and adjudication becoming more extensively used

Chapter 20
Legal Aspects of Tendering and Outsourcing

The following chapter contains a number of issues which have one theme acting as a common denominator – outsourcing. A general awareness of these issues is important even though they are not considered in great detail.

Issues to be considered in this lesson include:

- Specific & general tenders – a legal interpretation of the process
- The EC Procurement Directives & UK Regulations on public sector tendering
- The Acquired Rights Directive (98/50) & TUPE Regulations 1981
- Some practical implications of outsourcing from a legal perspective
- Redundancy & entitlement to compensation

Tenders

Almost all adverts requesting tenders to be submitted for the supply of goods or services are regarded as invitations to treat. The tenders themselves are seen as the offers, capable of being accepted or rejected by the buyer involved.

There are two types of tender:

- specific tenders i.e. one off transactions (quantity/delivery etc fixed and known in advance)
- general tenders (orders to be submitted if and when the goods/services are required - no fixed quantities/deliveries etc -

otherwise known as framework agreements)

With specific tenders, a binding contract comes into existence as soon as the successful tender is accepted. Both parties then have to fulfil their obligations to supply and pay for the goods/work done.

With the approval of a general tender, the offer is said to stand and will only be changed into a contract when an order is submitted. Each order is seen as an acceptance of this standing offer and separate contracts are concluded over the coming weeks or months. It is therefore possible for the firm who submitted the tender to revoke the offer at any time, although they will still have to perform any existing contracts agreed before the revocation.

Sometimes the firm which has submitted the tender commit themselves for a stated period of time but this will only be binding if consideration has been given in return or a deed (which does not require consideration) was concluded and signed.

Duties of the Buyer

- There is no obligation to accept any tender at all (unless this is stated at the time)

- There is no obligation to accept the lowest tender (unless this is stated at the time)

- There is no obligation to order goods or services under a general tender. If the buyer has promised to obtain the specified goods only from the successful tenderer, he cannot however go elsewhere during the period in question.

- There is no general obligation to order in line with suggested estimates referred to at the negotiation stage.

- There is a legal obligation to give due consideration to all properly submitted tenders which are received by any set deadline (Blackpool BC case)

- The process of awarding tenders is subject to a fundamental test of reasonableness. There can be exceptional circumstances where the procedure that was followed shows a degree of unfairness which the courts will find unacceptable (Camelot Case)

Blackpool & Fylde Aero Club Ltd v Blackpool Borough Council

The Aero club submitted a tender just before the deadline by placing it in the postbox at the town hall. However, the box was not opened by the council until several hours later. The council refused to consider the submission on account of it being passed the deadline. **HELD**: The council was in breach of the above implied undertaking and liable to pay damages.

Camelot Group Plc v National Lottery Commission (2001)

The National Lottery licence initially awarded to Camelot had run its seven years. Tenders had been requested by the Commission for the award of a new seven year licence. Two contractors submitted bids – Camelot and the People's Lottery (TPL). Having announced that both bids were considered unsatisfactory, the Commission decided that a new process would operate. There would be only one bidder – TPL. Camelot challenged this decision.

HELD: The action of the Commission (in deciding to negotiate exclusively with TPL) was so unfair as to amount to an abuse of power. It fell outside the range of decisions which a reasonable and properly informed decision-maker would take.

The EC Procurement Directives

A number of initiatives have been introduced since the start of the 1980's with the intention of increasing competition in public sector contracting. Compulsory competitive tendering (CCT) in local government was established in 1980 and subsequently developed to include such diverse activities as cleaning, refuse collection and disposal, security, finance, information technology services and housing management. Alternative arrangements for encouraging competitive tendering were also adopted in central government during this period. At the same time, a separate (and yet, clearly connected) development took place in the European Union with the passing of the Procurement Directives.

The Procurement Directives were aimed at encouraging free competition between member states - to create a level playing field. It was felt that too many contracts were awarded to suppliers based in the same country as the contracting organisation. This amounted to a form of domestic protectionism and was counter to the aims of the European Union and resulted in inefficiencies in the relevant market. The basic objective of the Directives is 'to ensure that all companies in the European Community have a fair chance in seeking contracts with public purchasing organisations.'

Who is affected by the Procurement Directives?

The Directives only relate to the public sector. Public purchasers comprise:

- Central government (departments of state & agencies)
- Local authorities
- Public utilities
- Other public bodies

There has been some dispute over whether the privatised 'public utilities' (water, gas, electricity, telecommunications etc) should have come within the ambit of the Directives. However, it has been justified on the grounds that they possess 'special or exclusive' rights in their respective sectors.

In the UK, the Directives have been implemented by the passing of a series of Regulations giving effect to their provisions:

- Public Works Contracts Regulations 1991 (SI 1991/2680)
- Public Supply Contracts Regulations 1995 (SI 1995/201)
- Public Services Contracts Regulations 1993 (SI 1993/3228)
- Utilities Regulations 1996 (SI 1996/2911)

A new unifying Directive (bringing together the three Directives on supplies, services and works and introducing some reform measures) will have to be implemented by early 2006.

The Directives are concerned with three issues relating to public sector procurement.

- Transparency of procedures

- Freedom of movement of goods & services
- More effective competition

How the Directives Operate

The Directives only apply where the contract is above a specified financial threshold (the figure varies, depending on the nature of the contract). A review of the threshold is carried out every two years. Where applicable, the Directives set out required procedures for tendering. These procedures, amongst other things, require:

- Minimum time limits for advance information notices, the tender period and the contract award notice
- The use of objective & non-discriminatory criteria when evaluating the tenders
- The procedures include a requirement that the contract must be advertised in the Official Journal of the European Union (OJEU). Various tender procedures are permitted under the Directives (open, restricted, & negotiated) but with significant restrictions relating to when negotiated procedure can be used.

Effect of non-compliance with the Directives

Suppliers with an interest in the contract can take legal action in the High Court. An interested supplier is an undertaking which sought (or would have wished) the awarding of the contract. It must also be a national of and established in a member state.

Once an action has commenced, the Court can:

- Suspend the procedure (or the implementation of any decision) if the contract has yet to be awarded
- Suspend the performance of the contract until the alleged infringement has been examined where the contract has already been awarded

- Issue orders requiring an infringing organisation to comply with the requirements

Remedies

At the end of the hearing, the Court can:

- Set aside the decision where a contract has yet to be awarded, and/or
- Award damages to the supplier who has brought the action

If the contract has already been awarded, only damages can be provided to the claimant supplier. However, the Court can issue orders requiring compliance (as above)

TUPE & Outsourcing

The TUPE Regulations 1981 implemented the requirements of a European Community Directive - the Acquired Rights Directive (ARD). The purpose of the Directive was to prevent employers arranging their commercial & corporate affairs in such a way as to evade or limit their employment law liabilities. The Directive has been subsequently amended (1998) and the Regulations are expected to be amended in the near future.

The effect of these provisions is to transfer the contracts of employment of affected employees to the transferee where a business (or activity) is acquired (or transferred).

The contracts of employment are not just preserved – the existing terms and conditions are protected. This means that previously unpaid wages are recoverable from the new employer, potential claims for unfair dismissal and discrimination and negligence against the transferor are transferred to the transferee. Previous continuous service will count for purposes of statutory employment rights such as redundancy payments and maternity rights.

This can result in significant increased costs and liabilities for both transferor and transferee.

However, occupational pensions are not transferred to the new employer.

Some Basic Points

The Regulations do not apply in the following situations:

- When the undertaking is not in the UK
- When the transfer is by way of transfer of shares in a company so that the only change is the identity of the shareholders and not the identity of the employing company
- When the transfer is a transfer of assets only, for example, the sale of a building, where all the employees of the seller continue to work for the seller in a different building

Types of Transaction affected

- Transfer (whether by sale or otherwise) of a business or part of a business as a going concern

- Contracting out of a service previously provided in house: the transferor will be the party requisitioning the services, the transferee the provider of them

- Transfer of a contract for services from one contractor to another: the transferor will usually be the outgoing contractor and the transferee the incoming one, where the contracts are back to back

- Bringing a service which was previously contracted out back in house: the transferor will be the provider of the services, the transferee the party taking then back in house

- Transfer of a franchise

- Transfer of a lease or licence

When does TUPE apply?

This has become one of the most difficult issues affecting employment law in recent years. The provisions contained in the ARD and TUPE need to be interpreted, a responsibility carried out by the European Court of Justice (ECJ) and the English courts, in particular, the Employment Appeal Tribunal (EAT). Over the years, the body of case law attempting to interpret the provisions has become increasingly confused, with very little consistency being maintained. The basic test is to ask the question:

Was a stable economic entity transferred?

For many years this was assumed to be largely determined by whether the same (or a similar activity) was continued after the transfer. This emphasis clearly suggested that contracting out came within the provisions. Then, in 1997, the ECJ seemed to change the focus by requiring the transfer of significant assets (the Suzen case). Where the activity did not involve tangible assets (plant, machinery etc) 'significant assets' comprised the majority of the workforce. This meant that in certain areas of outsourcing (e.g. cleaning, security etc) it seemed possible to avoid TUPE by refusing to take on the existing workforce. Subsequent decisions have made this more difficult. By 2001 we have two distinct approaches operating in the courts with some decisions supporting the Suzen case, and others supporting the earlier approach looking at a wider number of issues including similarity of activity before and after.

As the President of the EAT has said :

> "There is no doubt that the position in law in relation to transfer of undertakings is in a mess." (President Morison in OCS Cleaning (Scotland) Ltd v Rudden 1999)

The position relating to outsourcing may soon become clearer however. The amended ARD (98/50) specifically identifies contracting out as potentially applicable to its requirements and it is expected that new TUPE Regulations will confirm this approach when drafted and put into effect.

Dismissal for ETO reasons

Regulation 8(1) makes it automatically unfair to dismiss an employee for a reason connected with a relevant transfer (i.e. one that is covered by the TUPE Regulations).

An exception is allowed where the dismissal is for **economic, technical or organisational reasons** entailing **"changes in the workforce" – Regulation 8(2)** (an **ETO reason**).

The meaning of this expression ("changes in the workforce") has proved difficult to interpret clearly but it seems to require changes in either the numbers employed or some re-definition of job functions. The problem is that although it may be argued that organisational reasons were behind dismissals they do not entail changes in the workforce. This makes it very difficult indeed for a transferee employer effectively to harmonise terms and conditions after a transfer. Simply changing pay rates or working conditions in themselves do not amount to changes in the workforce. The case of *Berriman v Delabole Slate Ltd (1985)* illustrates this problem well. An employee suffered a reduction in his weekly wage. He resigned and claimedconstructive dismissal. The Court of Appeal held that the dismissal was automatically unfair as there was no economic, technical or organisational reason entailing changes in the workforce. For a change in the workforce within the meaning of Regulation 8(2) there had to be a change in the **composition** of the workforce. As we have seen, this meant a change in numbers or possibly job functions.

Information & Consultation Requirements

The current obligations to inform and consult with affected employees when TUPE applies are found in the Collective Redundancies & Transfer of Undertakings (Protection of Employment)(Amendment) Regulations 1999.

Where a recognised trade union exists, employers must consult with the union representatives. If there is no recognised trade union involved, the employer must consult with elected employee representatives. Employers now have to take a pro-active role in ensuring proper elections. This includes ensuring that (as far as is reasonable practicable):

- the election is fair
- the number of representatives elected is sufficient to represent the interests of the workforce affected
- the term of office of the representatives is long enough for adequate consultation to take place
- no affected employee is unreasonably excluded from standing for election
- the election is held by secret ballot (& the votes counted)
- elected representatives have time off work to undergo training for their new role

Remedies for Non-Compliance

Compensation for breach of the information and consultation obligations has been increased in the case of redundancies to 90 days pay in all cases (previously, a lesser penalty of 30 days pay applied in respect of fewer redundancies, i.e. over 20 but less than 100) and in cases involving transfers, to 13 weeks pay (from 4 weeks).

However, these obligations do not apply where fewer than 20 employees are proposed to be dismissed.

Reform – A clearer picture?

As we have seen, the uncertainty whether TUPE applies to outsourcing may be reduced after new Regulations are drafted to come into line with the revised ARD 98/50. The revised Directive has clearly indicated that it can apply to contracting out situations. There are many contractors and organisations wishing to engage in outsourcing which may prefer a clear position even if it means that TUPE will always apply. Amongst other reasons, this should simplify the tender procedure with bids being considered on separate criteria more related to quality than cost and with the position being more transparent to all involved.

Key clauses to include in outsourcing contracts

The terms and conditions should contain provisions relating to:

- Charging structure and fees
- Contract management
- Change control
- Service level agreements (in detail)
- Performance measures
- Incentives not to fall short on performance
- Renewal procedures and exit provisions

Redundancy

Where outsourcing is taking place, there is a real possibility that existing employees may find that their contracts of employment are terminated. We have seen that TUPE might enable these employees to bring claims for either unfair dismissal or redundancy against either the transferor or transferee. The following section looks in outline at the law on redundancy.

The Employment Rights Act 1996

This Act provides a wide-ranging series of statutory rights for employees at work. They include:

- Unfair dismissal protection
- Maternity rights
- Minimum notice entitlement
- Time off work for specified activities
- Redundancy payments

Redundancy Payments

The last entitlement is based on the concept that an employee should receive compensation for loss of job security. It is not strictly there to provide a financial buffer in between jobs – the employee could find better paid employment the next day and still be entitled to the redundancy payment. The issue is that he or she is less secure in the new work and does not receive statutory protection until they have served minimum periods of continuous service (the length varying depending on which statutory right is involved).

An employee must satisfy three requirements to be entitled to a redundancy payment. There must be:

- Dismissal
- A redundancy situation
- A minimum period of continuous employment

1 Dismissal

There are three variations of dismissal which permit claims:

- Dismissal by the employer with or without notice
- Constructive dismissal (resignation following a breach of contract by the employer)
- Failure to renew a fixed term contract

2 Redundancy

There are three variations that can arise:

- Complete closure of an organisation
- Closure of one factory, branch, office or site, but the organisation's other work places continue

Problems of entitlement to redundancy payment can arise here where an employee is required to move from one site to another. The employee may be unwilling to move and insist on a redundancy payment instead. The rights of the two parties will depend on interpreting the contract and the extent to which the employee can be seen to be mobile. If there is an express mobility clause requiring such movement, the employee cannot claim redundancy. If it does not extend as far as the required move, a payment can be claimed.

O'Brien v Associated Fire Alarms

Employee working in Merseyside was ordered to transfer to Barrow. He refused and claimed a redundancy payment. The employment tribunal looked at his contract and could find no reference to mobility. **HELD**: It was an illegitimate order entitling him to resign (constructive dismissal). It was a redundancy situation – his old job was disappearing, and he possessed the minimum period of notice. He won his claim

Some employees are deemed to possess an implied duty of mobility – those in selling or marketing roles and staff occupying management responsibilities. Employers need to be careful here – the mobility requirement is limited to a test of reasonableness – and it would be far safer to draft an explicit clause into the contract.

Where, although there is no closure of any factory, office etc, there is a reduction in the needs of the organisation for work of a particular kind

Problems arise as to what is 'work of a particular kind'? The needs of businesses can require all employees to be adaptable to a reasonable extent and to develop new skills and competencies as the work develops. If an employee fails to adapt to changing circumstances to a reasonable extent, any dismissal may be seen as fair (on the grounds of incapacity) and not redundancy – the job still exists, even though it has changed some of its appearance.

North Riding Garages Butterwick

Senior management decided to change emphasis of work in chain of garages from repair/maintenance to car sales. Each garage manager was given minimum sales targets to meet. The manager of one garage failed to meet the target and, after warnings, was dismissed. He claimed redundancy - the needs of the employer for work of a particular kind (manager of repair/maintenance garage) had diminished. The employment tribunal held that the job still existed – that of being a manager of a garage. All that had changed was the stress being given to different aspects of that work. The manager had proved incompetent in one of those aspects – selling.

Redundancy & Outsourcing

In the context of outsourcing, if the number of employees needed to carry on the outsourced activity is fewer (possibly because of different working methods or greater use of capital equipment), those who find their contracts terminated may well have a claim for redundancy payment.

Offers of Alternative Employment

Employees, instead of being given notice of redundancy, will sometimes be offered alternative work – their existing work no longer being required. This could be caused by newer technology or diversification into different areas of business. Can an employee refuse to transfer to the new work and claim a redundancy payment? This depends on considering the suitability of the new job compared with the old one. Refusal to accept the offer of a suitable alternative job will render the employee unable to claim a redundancy payment.

What is suitable?

This is a matter of 'substantial equivalence' between the two jobs, taking into account:

- The type of work involved
- Pay levels
- Status of the two jobs
- Overtime opportunities
- Shift work requirements

- Fringe benefits
- Travelling time

Some degree of adaptability and moderate financial loss may be expected, depending on the circumstances of the business in question.

An offer of suitable alternative work can be reasonably refused on grounds such as ill-health, dependent relatives, schooling problems where a move to another area is involved.

3 Continuous Employment

The employee has to have been continuously employed by the employer for two years in order to claim a statutory redundancy payment – private schemes may allow for claims at an earlier stage.

The Payment

The compensation is calculated according to a formula based on three criteria:

- Age of employee at time of dismissal
- Length of continuous service
- Gross pay at time of dismissal
- For each year of relevant employment between the ages of 18-21 – compensation of 0.5 weeks pay
- For each year of relevant employment between the ages of 22-40 – compensation of 1 week's pay
- For each year of relevant employment above the age of 41 – compensation of 1.5 week's pay

A maximum of 20 years service is allowed under the formula. Gross pay above £270·00 per week is disregarded (the maximum pay is subject to annual review – this figure is accurate at the time of writing – Summer 2004) This means that the maximum payment under the statutory scheme is 20 x 1.5 x £270·00 i.e. £8100.

Information & Consultation Requirements

We have already found a number of procedural requirements laid out by Parliament – in the Collective Redundancies & Transfer of Undertakings (Protection of Employment)(Amendment) Regulations 1999. The details have already been outlined in the previous section on TUPE.

Selection for Redundancy

Although redundancy constitutes one the gateways of reasons that can justify dismissal (thereby avoiding potential claims for unfair dismissal), unfair selection procedures override this immunity and permit such claims. The procedure must be fair and reasonable both in the way the process is conducted and the criteria used to decide selection. Certain criteria are treated as automatically unfair and include:

- Sex, race or disability discrimination
- Pregnancy, childbirth or maternity leave

- Trade union representation (or health & safety representation)

In other cases, the claim is decided on the reasonableness of:

- Selection of employees, or
- Procedure adopted

1 Selection

Employers are given a fairly free hand in choosing selection criteria provided that the pool from which the redundant employees will be selected is fair and the selection criteria are:

- Reasonably objective
- Not in breach of an agreed procedure (with, for example, a trade union)
- Fairly applied

The use of LIFO (last in/first out) is attractive to unions and employees because of its complete objectivity. It can however perpetuate weaknesses such as an ageing workforce. LIFO can be used effectively as a tie-breaker when other criteria result in a tie.

The most common selection criteria include the following:

- Skills & experience for remaining jobs
- Key skills
- Performance records
- Absenteeism/length of absence
- Disciplinary record

Criteria referred to in a staff handbook may give rise to claims for breach of contract if not implemented at a time of selection

Care has to be taken to ensure that the criteria chosen do not infringe the law on discrimination. Selecting part-time staff ahead of full-timers has been held to be indirect sex discrimination. Even 'length of service' has been challenged on the same grounds. The employer needs to be able to show there is objective neutral justification for choosing these criteria.

Deciding the Pool

i.e. deciding who are the affected employees (those within the job categories or departments from which the redundancies have to be made).

Adherence to an agreed procedure or custom and practice is usually a starting point. Ultimately, the decision has to satisfy the test of reasonableness in the circumstances. It may be appropriate to combine two sites or departments into a single 'pool'.

2   Procedure

The case of *Williams v Compair Maxim Ltd* identified three steps which should be taken when implementing redundancies. These are separate to any requirements relating to collective redundancies (see later). They are:

- To give as much advance warning as is reasonably practicable
- To consult with individual employees affected
- To consider opportunities to offer alternative suitable vacancies

Unfair Dismissal & Redundancy - Remedies

Where an employee is unfairly dismissed during a redundancy process, the normal remedy awarded by an employment tribunal is compensation. The alternatives of reinstatement or re-engagement are not usually awarded in order to avoid the consequence of another employee then being dismissed when the successful applicant returns to the organisation.

The current maximum award for unfair dismissal at present is £55,000 unless discrimination is involved where no maximum is set.

Collective Consultation

We have already found a number of procedural requirements laid out by Parliament – in the Collective Redundancies & Transfer of Undertakings (Protection of Employment)(Amendment) Regulations 1999. The details have already been outlined in the previous section on TUPE.

Where 20 or more employees are proposed to be made redundant within a period of 90 days, specific rules apply requiring to employer to carry out a consultation exercise. This must be undertaken 'with a view to reaching agreement' i.e. it must represent a genuine attempt by the employer. It is not a duty to negotiate – only to inform and provide an opportunity for alternative options to be put forward. The consultation must cover:

- Ways of avoiding the dismissals
- Ways of reducing the numbers to be dismissed
- Ways of mitigating the consequences of dismissal e.g. severance pay

Practical Alternatives

- Restrictions on recruitment
- Retirement of employees beyond normal retirement age
- Reductions in overtime
- Short-time working to cover temporary fluctuations
- Retraining
- Transfer to alternative work

Some consideration should be applied to the above options even if they have little likelihood of implementation (evidence in defence in subsequent claims)

The employer must provide the following information:

- The reason for the collective redundancy
- Numbers & descriptions of the employees the employer proposes to dismiss as redundant

- Proposed method of selection
- Proposed procedure for carrying out the redundancies
- Proposed method of calculating any redundancy payment in excess of the statutory redundancy payment

Having read this chapter, you should now have an understanding of the following issues and principles:

- Requests for tenders amount to an invitation to treat
- Tenders amount to offers
- With specific (one-off) tender agreements, the contract is agreed from the start – when the successful contractor is informed
- With general (as and when) tender agreements, contracts come into existence when individual call-offs are made – there is no continuing contract for the overall period in question
- Organisations must give proper consideration to all tenders that have been correctly submitted within the time scale set (the Blackpool BC case)
- The awarding of tenders is subject to a requirement that the process satisfies a basic level of fairness (the Camelot case)
- Public sector tendering procedures are regulated by EC Directives and UK Regulations intended to create a more free and transparent market between member states. Various enforcement powers are held by the courts to deal with any transgression
- The ARD & TUPE are intended to protect employees from losing their employment in the event of take-overs, mergers or outsourcing of activities. Their existing terms and conditions are preserved after the transfer. The legal position on when the Regulations apply to outsourcing is, however, very unclear at the present time
- Redundancy payments may be claimable when jobs are lost where an activity is being outsourced. Entitlement to a payment is based on rules set out in the Employment Rights Act 1996

- The process for redundancy and selection criteria used must be fair and reasonable. Otherwise, a claim for unfair dismissal will be available against the organisation involved.

Chapter 21
Insurance Law

Insurance law is a combination of general principles of contract and mercantile practice developed over the past centuries. The latter was legally recognised initially through the law merchant and later became incorporated into the common law. There have been very few Acts of Parliament relating to the topic, chiefly the Marine Insurance Act 1906.

Important sources of information to understand the parties' rights and obligations are always the documents of insurance – the proposal forms and policies.

The chapter examines the following legal principles and issues:

- Classification of insurance – distinction between property/liability insurance and life insurance
- Definition of insurance and its essential ingredients
- Formation and duration of insurance policies
- Meaning of 'insurable interest'
- Effect of fraud, misrepresentation, non-disclosure and breach of warranties
- Meaning and significance of 'uberrimae fidei'
- Meaning and significance of 'increase of risk' clauses
- Warranties and 'basis of contract' clauses
- Promissory warranties
- Subrogation

Types if Insurance

The most basic distinction in types of policy divides policies into:

- Property & liability insurance, &
- Life
- Property and liability insurance

The insurance company indemnifies (reimburses) the insured for the loss incurred. The policy does not specify in advance what the amount will be (although a maximum figure will be stipulated). The policy will compensate only for the loss actually suffered. Examples include fire, theft and marine insurance.

Liability insurance involves the insured being covered against the risk of claims by third parties. This covers potential actions for breach of contract and negligence and includes consequential losses.

Life insurance

Here the policy provides an agreed payment upon the happening of a specified event – a contingency event. The policy stipulates in advance how much will be paid. It is not based on actual loss suffered. For this reason it has been traditional to use the expression "assurance" instead of insurance. However, the two are used flexibly today and are frequently interchangeable.

Definition of Insurance

There is no statutory definition of insurance. One standard attempt suggests that a contract of insurance:

'is a contract to pay money or provide a service on the occurrence of a future uncertain event or a certain event, the date of which is uncertain, provided that the insured has an interest in that event.'

Three ingredients seem to be required:

1   Consideration

In exchange for periodical payments (premiums) the insured will be entitled to receive payment upon the happening of a specified event(s).

2   The event must be uncertain – either as to whether it will happen (fire, flood, accident etc) or when it will happen (death)

3   The insured must have an insurable interest in the uncertain event i.e. it will affect him adversely (e.g. as owner of the property damaged or stolen, or as a seller with a retention of title clause. Otherwise it would be deemed a wager and unlawful.

Authority to conduct business as an Insurer

It is an offence to conduct insurance business without the proper authorisation. This is achieved by obtaining a licence from the Department of Trade & Industry (or by being a Lloyd's Underwriter). There are minimum capital requirements and a stipulated excess of assets over liabilities. There are further requirements including adequate re-insurance arrangements.

Formation of the Contract

The general rule relating to simple contracts applies to insurance – they can be created in writing or orally. There is a requirement with life assurance policies for the assured to be sent a statutory notice before or at the time the contract is being concluded giving him or her the opportunity to change their mind and cancel the agreement.

The offer will normally come from the applicant; the acceptance from the insurance company. With renewals of property or liability insurance, the offer will usually be made by the insurer (by sending a reminder with details of premium to be paid etc). The insured will then accept by sending payment.

Cover notes are fully effective and treated as valid contracts of insurance. The only details that must be clear when the note is issued are the duration of the policy, the nature of the risk, and the premium to be paid. Most cover notes will state that they are issued subject to the standard terms and conditions of the insurer's usual policy. This attaches those terms to the arrangement with the insured.

Duration of the Contract

Leaving aside life assurance policies, most other contracts are for a fixed period of one year. A new contract must then be entered each time it is renewed. This imposes on the insured a further obligation to disclose changes in material facts between policies. The insurance company is under no obligation to renew a policy, nor to provide reasons for non-renewal. Most contracts contain conditions (for definition of this expression - see later) allowing the insurer to terminate the contract. They often relate to undertakings given by the insured such as to maintain the property insured in a reasonable state.

Once the insurer has incurred risk under the policy it will not be possible for the insured to recover any premium(s) paid under the policy. If, however, the policy becomes defective through operative mistake or misrepresentation by the insurer, he will be able to recover monies already paid to the insurer on the grounds of a total failure of consideration. The same is true where the insurance company avoids the contract for misrepresentation or failure to disclose on the part of the insured. The only exception is where the insured acted fraudulently.

Insurable Interest

One of the essentials of a contract of insurance is that the insured must have an insurable interest in the event insured against.

Again, we shall be only considering non-life insurance because of its greater relevance to the business world.

There are few issues of concern here when dealing with liability insurance. The applicant will always have an interest in protecting himself against potential liability to pay compensation to a third party.

However, problems occasionally arise when considering property insurance. One 'definition' of insurable interest is to require the applicant to have " a right in the property, or a right derivable out of some contract about the property." (Lord Eldon in Lucena v Craufurd). Simply being affected by loss or damage to property does not give the applicant sufficient standing. If, for example, a café owner whose business depended heavily on a nearby factory attempted to insure against the factory's damage or destruction, he would lack the necessary insurable interest.

Mere possession of property is not enough, unless it is being held as a bailee who has legal obligations to take reasonable care of its condition.

A leading case on insurable interest is:

Macaura v Northern Assurance Company Ltd

M. transferred his ownership in some timber forest land to a registered company he had recently formed. It was essentially a one-man company – he was the sole shareholder. He applied for a fire insurance policy to cover the land in question but put down his own name on the policy. A fire subsequently destroyed much of the forest. When he claimed on the policy it was held that he did not possess an insurable interest in the land. It was owned by the company, and although he was a shareholder (and creditor) of the company, this did not give him any rights to claim.

Where property insurance is involved, the applicant must have the insurable interest from the date on which the policy commences. It must also identify the name(s) of any other persons who are to be covered e.g. a tenant under a policy being concluded by the landlord.

Where goods are the subject matter of the policy, it is not necessary for the applicant to have an insurable interest in the strict sense when the contract is agreed. Some other form of interest in the goods is required – some potential loss from their destruction. This facilitates a whole range of business situations where goods are being held without ownership, yet the possessor may need insurance protection e.g. goods delivered on retention of title terms, goods received on hire or hire purchase terms.

When can the insurance company treat the policy as void?

Various events can allow the insurer to avoid the contract:

- Fraud
- Other forms of misrepresentation
- Non-disclosure of material information
- Breach of warranties

Fraud

If the applicant commits fraud on the proposal form, the contract can be treated as void by the insurer.

Misrepresentation

In theory, the normal rules of misrepresentation apply to insurance contracts. The insurer has the right to avoid the contract for any mis-statement of material facts by the proposer. In practice, insurance companies tend to treat such mis-statements either as non-disclosure and therefore covered by the doctrine of non-disclosure (see next) or as breach of warranty when they are found on the proposal form (see later)

Non-Disclosure

Contracts of insurance are an example (the most important example) of a class of contracts described as being uberrimae fidei. This translates as 'of the utmost good faith'. One party is in a far better position to know material facts than the other (i.e. the insured will possess the salient facts such as previous medical record, or the previous record of applications for similar policies etc.). In such cases, the law imposes a fiduciary duty (essentially placing the insured in a position of trust) on the applicant and requires him to disclose all material facts. If misleading (false) information is given, the contract is voidable and can be cancelled by the insurance company when the truth becomes known. It may not even have to return the existing premiums if it involves fraud or illegality. A classic case illustrating this principle is:

London Assurance Co v Mansel

When completing a life assurance policy, M. was asked whether he had made previous applications on his life. He replied that he was already insured at two offices, omitting to say that he had been declined at a number of other offices.

HELD: This was a failure to disclose a material fact, allowing the insurer to avoid the policy.

Whether an omitted fact is material or not is a question of fact and each case will have to be considered on its own merits. A case which concluded that the contract could not be set aside is:

Mutual Life Assurance Co (New York) v Ontario Metals Co

When asked for the name of any doctor consulted during the past 5 years, the applicant stated "None". This was untrue – he had consulted a doctor who had simply prescribed him a tonic. He had had no time off work. When the doctor's opinion was subsequently sought, he indicated that, if asked, he would have recommended acceptance of the risk by the insurer. **HELD:** No material fact was involved in this non-disclosure. The policy could not be avoided by the insurer.

In contracts uberrimae fidei:

- the applicant can commit misrepresentation by silence. If he fails to disclose important information (material to the contract) the contract can be avoided just as much as if the applicant had told a positive untruth.

- he commits a misrepresentation even when it was true at the time he originally made it but became inaccurate between then and when the insurance contract was concluded.

The duty of disclosure will normally operate in practice in connection with questions to be answered on the proposal form. It does however apply to the contract as a whole. Where insurance cover is to be renewed (yearly in most cases) there is a fresh obligation to disclose each time the contract is concluded.

Lambert v CIS Ltd

A wife had insurance cover for jewellery belonging to herself and her husband. The policy had been renewed for eight years. In 1971 her husband was imprisoned for dishonesty, a fact she did not disclose when renewing the policy in 1972. Later that year, she claimed for the theft of the jewellery. **HELD:** The insurer had the right to avoid the policy and refuse payment.

The duty to disclose only applies to material facts. The test to decide which facts are material is:

Would a reasonable insurer regard the fact in question as significant to his decision to agree the policy or to determine the amount of the premium?

Some facts by their very nature will be treated as clearly material. Examples include the previous history of applications for insurance by the proposer and his previous criminal record. Non-disclosure of a bad accident record or a high risk occupation are other examples.

The duty of non-disclosure was originally created in the context of marine insurance, when communications were poor and it was necessary to impose additional obligations on the party that possessed all the relevant information. It therefore pre-dated the evolution of proposal forms. In what ways do these forms affect the doctrine of uberrimae fidei? :

There is a presumption that information provided in answers to questions on the form are material to the insurance contract.

Where the insurer does not require further information to partially answered questions or those left blank, there is an inference that it is waiving any rights to claim non-disclosure subsequently.

Where questions are asked in specific terms, this limits the field of reference and the applicant is under no obligation to provide information outside that field. If, for example the question asks for details relating to the last 5 years, events from an earlier time can be omitted. Again, this is treated as a waiver of rights by the insurer.

Once the contract has been concluded, there is no general obligation to inform the insurer about changes in material facts. However, this can be affected by the presence of 'increase of risk' clauses in the policy. Sometimes called 'promissory warranties', the insured is under a duty to disclose all matters which permanently affect the risk covered by the policy. An example is:

Farnham v Royal Insurance Co

Under a property damage policy, the outbuildings of a farm were covered. The farmer had informed the insurance company that metal containers were being stored in his barns. Without telling the insurer, he had then allowed welding work to be carried out in the barns. **HELD**: The farmer should have informed the insurer about this change of use under an increase of risk clause found in the contract. As a result, the insurer could avoid the policy.

Warranties and Conditions

Insurance contracts obviously contain a variety of terms, located in the proposal form and the policy document. Some of these terms have assumed a particular significance in insurance law and need to be considered more closely. They are:

- Warranties

- Conditions

It must be made clear at the start that their meaning in insurance law is different from their standard meaning in general principles of contract – in fact in some ways they contradict this traditional definition. Usually, warranties are defined as terms of relatively minor importance to a contract; conditions are defined as terms of fundamental importance. The remedies for breach are consequently greater for infringement of a condition. In insurance law, a warranty is considered to be more important than a condition.

Warranties

A term under which the insured promises that a particular state of affairs exists or will exist, such that if it is untrue (or becomes untrue), the insurer will have the right to avoid the contract. It is irrelevant whether the breach of warranty caused or contributed to the loss.

Warranties can relate either to the present – warranting that a particular state of affairs already exists – or to the future – warranting that a state of affairs will exist or continue to exist for some future time. The latter is called a promissory warranty. If it is becomes untrue, the insurer can avoid the policy from the date of breach.

Warranties can be established in a variety of ways:

It is common for the proposal form to contain a provision indicating that the questions and answers constitute the basis of the contract, and any untruths will invalidate the policy. The effect of this is to enable the insurer to avoid the contract even where the untruth does not relate to a material fact:

Dawsons Ltd v Bonnin

A lorry had been insured against fire and third party liability. In answer to the question 'State full address at which vehicle will usually be garaged', the insured had inadvertently identified their normal place of business in central Glasgow. In fact it was housed on the outskirts of Glasgow – if anything, a safer place. The proposal form finished by stating that it was to form the basis of the contract. **HELD**: The insurer was entitled to avoid the policy because of this incorrect information. The clause making such answers the basis of the contract made the information a warranty.

Questions requiring an opinion by the applicant are not treated as warranties e.g. a question requiring an answer "to the best of the proposer's knowledge and belief." However, statements relating to future events can become promissory warranties even if they do not amount to statements of fact at the time the proposal form is being completed:

Hales v Reliance Fire & Accident Insurance Co Ltd

When answering a question on the proposal form that asked whether any inflammable oils or goods were used or kept on the premises, a shopkeeper stated that 'lighter fuel' was the only such product. In the run-up to Guy Fawkes Night, he bought a stock of fireworks. This was held to be a promissory warranty that had been infringed from the moment the fireworks were delivered. The policy could be avoided by the insurer from that moment.

Where the clause uses the expression 'Warranty' or states that 'the insured warrants' it will be treated as a warranty.

Where a clause indicates that the happening or non-happening of a specified event will cause the contract to become void, it will be treated as a warranty.

Promissory warranties can lead to difficult problems of interpretation. If there is any ambiguity in the clause, it will be interpreted narrowly, against the wishes of the insurance company:

Provincial Insurance Company Ltd v Morgan

Coal merchants wished to insure a lorry and completed the proposal form. One of the questions required them to 'State (a) the purpose in full for which the vehicle will be used; and (b) the nature of the goods to be carried.' They answered "delivery of coal" and "coal" respectively. On one occasion, they transported some timber as well as coal. After delivering the timber and some of the coal there was an accident and they wished to claim on the policy. The insurance company argued that there was a breach of a promissory warranty. **HELD**: On a reasonable interpretation, the coal merchants had only warranted that the lorry would carry coal, which was accurate – not that it would carry coal exclusively.

Conditions

These are clauses that cover issues which are not fundamental to the risks covered by a policy and do not relate to statements of fact. They include terms giving the insurer additional rights beyond those provided by general principles. Examples are rights of cancellation and subrogation (see below).

Failure to comply with a condition in an insurance contract will only allow the insurance company to avoid a specific liability for a particular loss. Liability for other losses under the policy continue to apply where the relevant conditions have been satisfied.

Subrogation

This doctrine applies to insurance policies that have indemnified the insured against certain risks such as fire, motor, or non-payment of money (but not to life or personal accident insurance). It is designed to prevent the insured from being able to recover more than a full indemnity:

"The contract of insurance ... is a contract of indemnity, and of indemnity only, ... and the assured shall be fully indemnified, but shall never be more than fully indemnified." (*Castellain v Preston*)

The doctrine has two elements:

- The insured cannot make a profit from his loss
- The insurer has a right to step into the shoes of the insured (and, in his name, pursue claims which may reduce the loss insured against)

1   The insured cannot make a profit

An early example of this rule is found in:

Darrell v Tibbits

The owner of a house insured it against fire. It was leased to a tenant. Serious damage was caused to the building by an explosion caused by the local council. The council paid compensation to the tenant, who used the money to make good the repairs (as he was required to do under the tenancy agreement). The insurance company paid up under the fire policy and then sought to recover the money.

HELD: It was entitled to the return of the payment. The owner would have profited if he had been able to keep the insurance money (an example of double indemnity).

2   The right to take action

This will usually involve a right to sue a third party liable to pay damages in tort or for breach of contract:

Lister v Romford Ice & Cold Storage Ltd

A son and his father were employed as a driver and his mate. Whilst helping his son reverse the lorry, the father was injured by his son's negligent driving. The employer was held vicariously liable for the son's negligence and had to pay significant compensation. The money was in fact paid under the relevant insurance policy. The insurance company then insisted (as they were entitled to do under the terms of the policy) that a breach of contract claim be brought against the son – for breaching the implied duty to perform work competently and using reasonable care. There is an implied right in a contract of employment for an employer to be indemnified against losses caused by unlawful behaviour of employees

HELD: The insurance company was entitled to pursue this claim and secure the return of their money.

The insured must not do anything to prejudice the insurer e.g. by entering into a compromise with the wrongdoer:

West of England Fire Insurance Co v Isaacs

A sub-tenant insured property against fire. Following a fire, he claimed on the policy and received payment. He paid this money to the tenant to execute repair work. At the same time he undertook not to sue the tenant for a breach of the tenancy agreement – a covenant that the tenant would arrange suitable insurance cover himself. In fact he was under insured or the property in question.

HELD: The sub-tenant was liable to return the equivalent money to the insurance company. He had prejudiced their potential right to use his name to sue the tenant for breach of the covenant.

Another case illustrating this principle is:

Phoenix Assurance Co v Spooner

Mrs Spooner insured property belonging to her against fire. During the period in which the policy was covering the property, Plymouth Corporation served notice of a compulsory purchase order. Shortly afterwards, the property was destroyed in a fire. Phoenix paid £925 under the policy. Subsequently, Mrs Spooner negotiated an arrangement with the council by which it paid her the difference between the price she would have received if the property had been intact and the £925 she had received under the insurance policy. Phoenix argued that it was entitled to recover the £925 from Mrs Spooner.

HELD: At the time of the fire, the risk had already transferred to the council. Mrs Spooner should therefore have been entitled to the full purchase price. As Phoenix were subrogated to Mrs. Spooner's rights, they could claim the return of the money from her.

In conclusion:

- Insurance can be broadly classified into policies covering property or liability and policies covering life

- The three essential requirements for a valid insurance policy are consideration uncertainty of the event and an 'insurable interest' possessed by the applicant

- Various factors can invalidate insurance policies, chiefly non-disclosure of material information and breach of warranties

- Insurance contracts are an example of contracts uberrimae fidei (of the utmost good faith), imposing stricter requirements on the applicant to disclose material information

- Increase of risk clauses can require the insured to update the insurance company on any changes of material importance which permanently affect the risk covered

- Breach of a 'warranty' as defined in an insurance contract entitles the insurance company to terminate the contract

- Insurance companies can 'step into the shoes' of the insured to claim rights using the doctrine of subrogation

Appendix 1
Answering Case Studies in Law Examinations

There is a tendency amongst candidates taking the Professional Stage examinations to regard Legal Aspects as one of the more difficult modules to pass. There are a number of reasons, which have led to this view – the lack of day to day contact with the subject matter - the more abstract nature of many of the principles and concepts involved. As a result many candidates lack basic confidence which sometimes affects performance. But one of the unfortunate and unnecessary features of their taking the module can be a basic ignorance of how law papers are marked – the methodology for assessing papers and allocating marks. There is in fact a distinctive technique, which, if understood, will substantially improve your chances of success.

Process, more than Conclusions

Although drawing up valid and appropriate conclusions is clearly an important element of answering law questions, the bulk of the marks are not awarded in this area. Most are awarded for the setting out of a series of stages by which suitable conclusions can be drawn. An analogy can be made to the taking of a Maths exam. Let us assume 2 students are answering a maths question worth 20 marks. Student A writes down nothing on the answer sheet except the correct answer. Result – he or she fails. Student B explains how they move through a series of stages, citing appropriate formulae and principles. However, near the conclusion, a simple arithmetical mistake is made and the wrong answer is reached. Result – a pass (possible with distinction if the rest of the answer is well presented and explained. The same approach applies to law questions.

Avoid conclusions until the end

There is a natural tendency to jump straight into a case study or problem and start discussing the rights and duties of the parties involved. This is dangerous because you will tend to assume knowledge of the basic legal principles and merely apply them.

Remember – the bulk of the marks are awarded for the identification and explanation of the relevant legal principles.

(N.B. When drawing your conclusions, marks can be awarded for introducing practical ideas and approaches, which reinforce your legal analysis. Remember though – these should only supplement the legal points, not replace them)

Answering a law problem

To avoid the above danger , the following technique is suggested:

Stage One

Read scenario and identify relevant legal issues and principles. Produce a rough list, including any statutes and cases, which come to mind.

Stage Two

Without referring to the problem, explain as fully as possible the above legal principles.

In doing so, refer to relevant legislation (including section numbers for important provisions) and case law (see later)

Stage Three

Apply the above explanation to the problem now. Draw appropriate conclusions if you can (rights/duties of the parties). Indicate when you cannot do this and the reason(s) why e.g. insufficient information in the scenario; uncertainty in the law itself.

How do you use cases?

Candidates often become anxious about revising cases – how many need to be committed to memory; what do I need to memorise; what do I do if I can't remember the name of a case. Whilst it is true to say that cases must always be studied as part of a preparation for any law exam, a balance needs to be drawn so that you can still see the wood for the trees –spending all you time learning details of cases, many of which are not of great importance to the development of the law, can cause unnecessary anxiety. You therefore need to focus on two types of case:-

- **landmark cases** – those, which have had a fundamental impact on legal development. There are nearly always one or two such cases in each major topic in the syllabus. Some examples are Hadley v Baxendale (awarding of unliquidated damages); Taylor v Caldwell (doctrine of frustration of contract); Donoghue v Stevenson (negligence liability).

- **recent cases** which have been decided in the last few years and which show you have the ability to keep updated in the law as it continues to develop.

Remember too that cases are not important for their facts – they are important for the legal principles which they created or are illustrating. Yes, include the facts of a landmark case, which is central to your problem, but try to relate it clearly to the principle of law involved. With cases of smaller importance, just refer to the mane and say that it illustrated the point of law being discussed. (And if you forget the name of that important case, just say "In an actual case ..." and continue as you intended. You should not be penalised and you have shown a certain subtlety of approach. Do not try to remember the years when cases were decided – unless there is a particular significance to this fact e.g. it is a recent case and casts doubt on earlier cases on the same issue. on the same issue.

Getting to grips with Case Studies

For the longer "problem" found in Section A of the Legal Aspects paper – the case study – it is important to become very familiar with the scenario. One technique I would thoroughly recommend is to convert it into a diagram – make it more visual by creating an overview on an single sheet of A4 – names of parties in capitals and circled, events noted in concise form, arrows leading from company to company etc. Try not to clutter the page – leave as much white space as possible. Then list the potential legal principles in a column to one side – a word or short note representing each one. This activity forces you to become more aware of all the issues involved.

Constructing the Answer

Always prepare a rough plan. To those who protest insufficient time I would suggest you consider how much time is spent stopping and starting between points when no clear plan has been produced at the beginning of the answer. By creating a rough plan, a number of benefits result. You cast your mind wider before becoming locked into specific issues and therefore tend to remember more. You become aware of what is coming later in your answer – which helps your presentation of ideas. You write continuously which improves the fluency of your style.

For these reasons, the following technique is suggested:-

■ Read the question closely (and establish what it is really asking – not the question you have prepared for and would like it to be asking)

- List all the legal points and principles you feel to be relevant until you cannot add to it

- Re-read the question and check if all the points are relevant.

- Re-arrange the remaining points into a better sequence – one which answers to question more directly

- Decide which of the points are 'core' issues, which need to be developed more fully. Asterisk them to remind yourself as you start to write the answer in full

This takes time, but remember, you will make up for this later. And you will be convincing the examiner that you are an intelligent candidate capable of adapting the material to the needs of the question.

Some basic exam guidance

Draw up a timetable   Remember that in addition to testing your knowledge and understanding of a subject, exams are testing your ability to use a limited amount of time efficiently and effectively. You must therefore plan how much time you have for each question and sub-question. Look at the weighting next to the questions for help here.

Best questions first.   Tackle the questions in descending order of preference. Go for your best one at the start and gain the confidence a good start can provide. This could well be from Section B of the paper – it does not matter in which order you answer the questions from the examiner's point of view.

Provide ammunition.   Remember that the examiner is on your side and will want to find marks from you script. Therefore, give him/her the opportunity to locate them by answering all the questions and sub-questions you are required to answer or have chosen to answer. Do not opt out of any because you don't think you know enough. There are always some 'easy' marks going at the start of each answer and you may well be able to pick them up by writing generally about the topic. Therefore – always provide the examiner with ammunition by having a go at all the relevant questions.

Final Thoughts

Exam technique often requires you to do things, which do not come naturally in the heat of exam conditions. Producing plans before answering the question, avoiding the problem until you have fully set out the principles first, carefully devising a timetable at the start to indicate where you should be for the rest of the time – none of these come easily at the time they are most needed. You should therefore develop these approaches over a period of time and practice them in mock conditions or even when simply producing an answer to a coursework question. If you practise these recommended approaches, your standard of presentation will inevitably improve and with it your confidence and your chances of success.

Appendix 2

Example of Examination Technique – Approach to questions on Third Party Liability

Section A case studies will sometimes focus on the issue of third party liability. For example, the scenario could involve work being carried out on building new premises or renovating existing ones. The owner of the property engages a main contractor to carry out the work. Specialist work (electrical fittings, plumbing etc) may then be delegated to sub-contractors by the main contractor. Problems arise and the potential claims of the owner of the property have to be examined.

This requires candidates to demonstrate an understanding of the doctrine of privity of contract and the need sometimes to rely on alternative claims (non-contractual) against sub-contractors who have performed incompetent work.

The doctrine of privity states that only the parties to a contract have the right to sue for its breach. Third parties (organisations who were not parties to the contract but who may be affected by its performance) have no such ability even though they could suffer harm as a result of its defective performance – as with the property owner in the above scenario if a sub-contractor performs incompetent work.

To answer the relevant tasks accompanying the case study, it can be extremely useful to ask a number of questions. They relate to each of the contractors identified in the scenario. Assuming you are the claimant organisation:

1   Did you have a contract with the organisation?

Contractual claims are always easier to win. Liability is strict – simply failing to perform obligations which were promised is enough. There is no need to prove fault – that the contractor was in some way to blame for the breach. Clearly, the most likely target here is the main contractor with whom you negotiated a contract. The terms of this contract should clearly make the main contractor responsible for any faulty performance of sub-contractors. This should be in the form of warranties and indemnities obtained form the main contractor. It is also possible you made a contract with a consultant surveyor or architect – check the facts of the scenario here.

2   If a contract does exist, what type of contract is it?

You need to ask this question in order to know which law governs your rights. If it is a sale of goods contract, you can refer to the Sale of Goods Act 1979, in particular, sections 12 –15 and the implied rights of a buyer relating to the goods (satisfactory quality, fitness for purpose etc.). If it is a contract for work and materials (which is clearly more likely in building or renovation scenarios) or professional services, you should refer to the Supply of Goods and Services Act 1982 (Part One for the quality of materials supplied; Part Two for the competence of the work done).

If there is no explicit contract, can you discover an implied (collateral) contract?

This requires you to check the facts of the case study to see if any assurances were given during the negotiations by a business which caused you to insist on the purchase of their specific goods or materials by your contractors. Even if the scenario does not seem to include this possibility it is good technique to ask the question, explain briefly what is meant by a collateral contract and refer to a case in support – *Shanklin Pier Ltd v Detel Products Ltd* is a useful example.

4 If there is no explicit or implied contract, were you identified as a third party with rights?

This requires you to show an awareness of changes brought about by the Contracts (Rights of Third Parties) Act 1999, which came into force on 11th May 2000 and constitutes a major inroad to the doctrine of privity.

5 If none of the above apply, is there a non-contractual claim which gives you rights?

The two most likely claims here will be:

■ The tort of negligence

■ A statutory claim under the Consumer Protection Act 1987 (Part One)

This requires you to set out the essential ingredients for success. In negligence, you should identify the three requirements (duty of care, breach of duty, consequent damage). Spend some time explaining each one and be careful to consider the issue of claimable damage. Remember that although personal injury and damage to property is claimable in negligence, it is not normally possible to claim for purely economic loss (unless a nominated sub-contractor is involved). Therefore, lost orders and profits will not be recoverable in such claims.

Under Part One of the Consumer Protection Act 1987 you need to establish whether a consumer has sustained damage. If this is the case, you should outline the main provisions of the Act. These include the requirements for a successful claim and the parties who can be made liable, the meaning of 'dangerous' product, the meaning of 'damage' and the main defences available.

A useful additional point would be to ask if a collateral warranty had been obtained from the sub-contractor at the outset – a guarantee given in exchange for a payment (possible nominal) which entitles you to bring a direct contractual claim against the sub-contractor.

Appendix 3
Landmark Cases

This is a list of essential cases that you must have included in your revision for the CIPS examination in 'Legal Aspects'. It is not therefore a list representing all the cases you should know. Just how many more you include will depend on your available time and your need to feel well-placed on the eve of the examination.

Section A

Letters of Intent	BSC v Cleveland Bridge & Engineering Co
Invitation to Treat	Pharmaceutical Society of G.B. v Boots Cash Chemists
Counter Offer	Hyde v Wrench (& unconditional acceptance)
Communication of Acceptance	Felthouse v Bindley
Implied Acceptance	Brogden v Metropolitan Rly. Co
Battle of the Forms	Butler Machine Tool Co v Ex Cell O Ltd
Tenders	Blackpool & Fylde Aero Club v Blackpool Corporation
	Camelot Group Plc v National Lottery Commission

Consideration	Atlas v Kafco
	Williams & Co v Roffey Bros
Mistake	Scott v Coulson (or Couturier v Hastie)
Liquidated Damages	Dunlop Pneumatic Tyre Co v New Garage Ltd
Unliquidated Damages	Hadley v Baxendale
Misrepresentation	Hedley Byrne & Co v Heller & Partners
	Leaf v International Galleries
Exclusion (reasonableness)	George Mitchell v Finney Lock Seeds Ltd
Frustration	Taylor v Caldwell
Time of the Essence	Charles Rickards v Oppenheim
Instalment Deliveries (right to cancel all of contract)	Maple Flock Ltd v Universal Furniture Products Ltd
Privity of Contract	Dunlop v Selfridge
Collateral Contracts	Shanklin Pier Ltd v Detel Products Ltd
Negligence	Donoghue v Stevenson
	Hedley Byrne & Co. v Heller & Partners
	Simaan General Contracting Ltd v Pilkingtin Glass Ltd
	Junior Books Ltd v Veitchi Co Ltd

Section B

Competition Law

Article 81 infringement	Consten Grundig v Commission
Definition of dominant position	United Brands v Commission
Intra State effects on trade	Hugin v Commission
Article 82 infringement	Tetra Pak v Commission

IPR

Passing Off	Bollinger v Costa Brava Wine Co
Passing Off	Erven Warninck v Townend
Confidential Information	Saltman Engineering v Campbell
Confidential Information	Seager v Copydex Ltd
Confidential Information	Faccenda Chicken Co v Fowler
Design Right	British Leyland v Armstrong
Patents Ltd	

Insurance

Warranties ('basis of contract')	Dawsons Ltd v Bonnin
Promissory Warranties	
(ambiguity)	Provincial Insurance Ltd v
Morgan	
Subrogation	Phoenix Assurance v Spooner

Appendix 4
Legal Aspects - Revision Questions

For those readers studying for the Legal Aspects paper of the Professional Stage of the CIPS Graduate Diploma, or other law exams, the following list of questions will be useful as a revision aid. It is recommended that you study a particular legal topic and then look for the relevant questions in the list below and work through questions progressively in discrete sections.

Formation of Contract

- What is a contract (basic definition)?
- What are the legal differences between deeds and simple contracts?
- What are the essentials of a simple contract? (basic headings)
- What is the difference between void and voidable contracts (and what gives rise to each type of defective agreement)?
- Is a letter of intent legally binding?
- What happened in British Steel Corporation v Cleveland Bridge & Engineering Co Ltd10 and what was the outcome?
- What is meant by quantum meruit and when can it be useful to a contractor?
- What is an offer? (definition)
- What is an invitation to treat (definition) and give some examples?

- What happened in Fisher v Bell (or Pharmaceutical Society of G.B. v Boots Cash Chemists) and what was the outcome?

- In what ways can an offer terminate?

- What is the only correct way in which to accept an offer?

- What happened in Hyde v Wrench and what was the outcome?

- What is the effect of agreeing 'subject to contract' and why does it have this consequence?

- What happened in Felthouse v Bindley and what was the outcome?

- What happened in Brogden v Metropolitan Railway Co and what was the outcome?

- What is the postal rule of acceptance and when does it not apply to acceptances sent by post?

- What is meant by the battle of the forms and why is it important to win it?

- How can you link the previous section on offer and acceptance to the battle of the forms?

- What happened in Butler Machine Tool Ltd v Ex-Cell-O Corporation and what was the outcome?

- What happened in BRS v Arthur Crutchley Ltd and what was the outcome?

- What is meant by consideration in a simple contract?

- What are the requirements for valid consideration?

- What happened in Stilk v Myrick and Hartley v Ponsonby and what were the outcomes?

- What happened in Atlas v Kafco and what was the outcome?

- What is meant by duress and economic duress?

- What happened in North Ocean Shipping Co v Hyundai Construction (also known as 'The Atlantic Baron' case) and what was the outcome?

- What happened in Williams & Co v Roffey Bros and what was the outcome?

- Do mistakes normally invalidate contract and why?

- What examples can you give of operative (or fundamental) mistake and indicate any cases that may be given in support?

- What is meant by rectification

- What happened in Joscelyne v Nissen and what was the outcome?

- What is a misrepresentation? (a definition, broken down into its component parts)

- What remedies are available for fraudulent, negligent and wholly innocent misrepresentation? (include the legal sources for your response too)

- When is the remedy of rescission lost?

- What happened in Leaf v International Galleries and what was the outcome?

Content of Contract and Liability for Breach

- What is meant by 'express' terms and 'implied' terms?

- What is the difference between conditions and warranties and why is it necessary to know which is involved?

- What is meant by the expression 'innominate term' and why was it developed as a new way of helping to classify terms in a contract?

- What happened in the Hong Kong Fir Shipping case and what was the outcome?

- What is the effect of 'acceptance' of the goods on the remedies of a buyer who wished to claim breach of contract?

- When are goods deemed to be accepted according to the Sale of Goods Act 1979? (include reference to section numbers here)

- What are liquidated damages? (definition)

- What are their main advantages and disadvantage?

- What is a penalty? (definition)

- How can liquidated damages be distinguished from penalties? (identify the case that established the tests involved and the tests themselves)

- What is meant by unliquidated damages?
- What is the underlying purpose of an award of damages?
- What are the rules in Hadley v Baxendale?
- What happened in Victoria Laundry v Newman Industries and what was the outcome?
- What happened in Parsons (Livestock) Ltd v Uttley Ingham & Co and what was the outcome - what principle of law was illustrated here?
- What types of 'damage' can be claimed for in a breach of contract action?
- What happened in Lambert v Lewis and what was the outcome? (what principle of law was illustrated here)
- What happened in Anglia TV v Reed and what was the outcome? - what principle of law is being illustrated?
- What is meant by mitigation of loss and which case can be used to illustrate it in operation?
- What is meant by anticipatory breach?
- What is meant by an exclusion of liability?
- What two barriers to effectiveness of exclusion can you identify as being common law (judge-made) in origin?
- What happened in Olley v Marlborough Court Hotel and what was the outcome?
- What happened in Baldry v Marshall (or Andrews v Singer) and what was the outcome?
- How is exclusion of liability for negligence regulated by section 2 of the Unfair Contract Terms Act 1977?
- How is exclusion of liability for breach of contract regulated by section 3 of the Act?
- How is exclusion of liability for breach of the implied terms found in sale of goods contracts regulated by section 6 of the Act?
- What factors are identified in the Act as relevant in deciding whether an exclusion clause is fair and reasonable?
- What happened in George Mitchell v Finney Lock Seeds Ltd and what

was the outcome? (alternative cases - RW Green v Cade Bros Farm, or St Albans City & District Council v ICL)

- What is meant by frustration of contract? (definition of the doctrine and the effect it has on the contract)

- What are the main examples of events that can frustrate contracts?

- What happened in Taylor v Caldwell and what was the outcome?

- What happened in Avery v Bowden and what was the outcome?

- What happened in Chandler v Webster and what was the outcome?

- What happened in Metropolitan Water Board v Dick, Kerr & Co and what was the outcome?

- In what way can Davis Contractors v Fareham UDC be contrasted with the Water Board case?

- What are the consequences of the Law Reform (Frustrated Contracts) Act 1943 on contracts which have become frustrated?

- What is a force majeure clause? (definition)

- What are the main advantages to one or both parties of their inclusion in a contract?

- What is the relationship between force majeure clauses and the Unfair Contract Terms Act 1977?

Sale of Goods and Services

The Sale of Goods Act 1979 is an example of laissez faire legislation.

- What is meant by this statement?

- What are the five implied conditions found in the Sale of Goods Act 1979 and which sections apply?

- In what situation is it no longer possible (since1995) for a buyer to repudiate a contract for breach of the above implied conditions?

- What examples can you give of how section 12 can be broken?

- What examples can you give of how section 13 can be broken?

- What is meant by 'satisfactory quality'? (definition, including additional features added in 1995)

- In what types of contract does the Supply of Goods & Services Act 1982 imply a number of terms?

- What implied terms are attached by Part One of the Act?

- What implied terms are attached by Part Two of the Act?

- What happened in Charles Rickards v Oppenheim and what was the outcome? What principle of law is being illustrated?

- Why is it necessary to know when there has been a transfer of property (ownership) from seller to buyer?

- When does property in goods transfer?

- What is meant by Nemo Dat Quod Non Habet?

- What are the exceptions to the doctrine, including the relevant sections and any supporting case law?

- What are the rights of a buyer under the Sale of Goods Act 1979 where the wrong quantity is delivered? (including section number)

- What are the rules governing the right of a buyer to cancel the remainder of a contract for delivery by instalment where one delivery is in breach of contract?

Non Contractual Liability

- What principle of law was established in Dunlop v Selfridge and what does this principle (or doctrine) mean?

- What impact has the Contracts (Rights of Third Parties) Act 1999 had on this doctrine? What are its main provisions?

- What is meant by a collateral warranty?

- What is meant by a collateral contract and how does Shanklin Pier v Detel Products Ltd illustrate it in practice?

- What area of law do negligence claims form an example? (together with defamation, nuisance, deceit etc)

- When is a duty of care owed in the law of negligence:

- What happened in Donoghue v Stevenson and what was the outcome?

- What are good examples of duty of care relationships in commercial/financial activities?

- What happened in Hedley Byrne & Co v Heller & Partners and what was the outcome?

- When is a duty of care broken by a defendant & what factors are used to help determine the decision?

- Why are negligence claims difficult to win in court and how does the doctrine known as res ipsa loquitor help the claimant sometimes?

- What is meant by the 'but for' test when deciding damages in negligence actions?

- What types of 'damage' are claimable in negligence actions and what types are not?

- What happened in Simaan General Contracting Co v Pilkington Glass and what was the outcome? (or Spartan Steel & Alloys Ltd v Martin & Co)

- How did the case of Junior Books Ltd v Veitchi Co Ltd affect this position?

- Why was the Consumer Protection Act 1987 passed?

- What is the basic difference between this statutory claim and one brought in negligence?

- Who can be made liable under the Act?

- When is a product 'defective'?

- What 'damage' is recoverable under the Act?

- What is meant by the 'developmental risks' defence?

- How long is it possible to bring a legal action under the 1987 Act?

Agency

- What is meant by actual and apparent authority in the law of agency?

- Which is the more important when deciding whether a principal is bound by the actions of an agent?

- What is meant by ratification?
- What is the doctrine of the undisclosed principal?

Assignment

- What is meant by contractual assignment? What can and cannot be assigned in a contract?
- What is meant by novation?

Tenders

- What are the legal stages involved in a tender procedure?
- What are the implied (collateral) duties that attach to tendering procedures?
- What happened in Blackpool & Fylde Aero Club v Blackpool Borough Council and what was the outcome?
- What happened in Camelot Group plc v National Lottery Commission and what was the outcome?
- What is the purpose of the EC Procurement Directives?
- Which organisations are governed by their requirements?
- Which types of contract are regulated and when do the rules become relevant?
- What are the basic requirements that must be satisfied?
- What can happen if the Directives (&/or UK Regulations) are not observed correctly?

TUPE & Outsourcing

- What is the purpose of the Acquired Rights Directive and, consequently, the Transfer of Undertakings (Protection of Employment) Regulations 1981 (TUPE)?
- What is the basic legal consequence of TUPE?
- In what situations does TUPE become relevant

- Does TUPE apply to contracting out/contracting in arrangements?
- What is meant by 'ETO' reasons linked to a dismissal?
- What are the information and consultation requirements where TUPE applies to a transaction? What remedies are available for infringement?
- What contractual clauses would be useful to include in an outsourcing contract?

Redundancy

- What is 'redundancy'? (definitions)
- What is the difference between redundancy and severance?
- What are the 3 requirements for a successful redundancy claim?
- Does an employee have to accept an offer of alternative work to that which he has been doing?
- Re selection for redundancy, what cannot be used as criteria for selection without it being unfair dismissal?
- What factors can be taken into account in making the selection decision?
- What basic rules need to be observed to satisfy procedural fairness where redundancies are being carried out?
- What consultation requirements exist where collective redundancy is involved?
- What options exist as an alternative to redundancy?

Competition Law

- Why was the Competition Act 1998 passed?
- What is the basic distinction between Article 81 & Article 82 of the European Treaty (as to when they apply)?
- Re Article 81, what is meant by an 'undertaking'?
- Re Art 81, what is meant by an 'agreement'
- What are the main examples of anti competitive practice identified in

Article 81?

- What are 'horizontal' and 'vertical' agreements and how does this distinction affect the approach of the European Commission?

- What are the requirements regarding impact on trade for Article 81 to be infringed?

- What happened in Consten Grundig v Commission and what was the outcome?

- What are the requirements for an exemption to be obtained under Article 81?

- How is the relevant market analysed for purposes of Article 81?

- What is the difference between a block exemption & an individual exemption?

- What is meant by a 'comfort letter'?

- What is meant by a 'dominant position' for purposes of Article 82? (definition + reference to precedent case)

- What are the main examples of anti competitive practice identified in Article 82?

- Can you explain the facts and outcomes of the following cases - United Brands v Commission; Hugin v Commission; Tetra Pak v Commission?

- What are the enforcement powers of the European Commission regarding Articles 81 & 82?

- How does the Merger Regulation (Regulation 4064/89) deal with the issue of control of mergers in the European Union?

- How does the Enterprise Act 2002 (which has replaced the Fair Trading Act 1973) deal with the issue of monopolies and mergers in the UK? (Include definitions of 'monopoly' and 'merger')

- What are the similarities and differences between Articles 81 & 82 of the European Treaty and Chapters One and Two of the Competition Act 1998?

- What is the role and modus operandi of the following competition law agencies - the European Commission; the Office of Fair Trading; the Competition Commission; the Department of Trade & Industry?

International Trade

- Why were INCOTERMS established and when do they attach to a contract of sale?

- What are the responsibilities of the seller and buyer in a CIF contract?

- When does ownership and risk pass?

- What are the responsibilities of the seller and buyer in a FOB contract?

- When does ownership and risk pass?

- What is meant by FOB with additional services?

- What differences exist between FOB contracts and FAS contracts?

- What are the responsibilities of the seller and buyer in an ex works (EXW) contract? When does ownership and risk pass?

- What is meant by DDP and who is responsible for what?

- What is a bill of lading? (definition)

- What 3 characteristics does a bill of lading possess?

- What different forms of bill are used in practice?

- What is a charterparty?

- What is the purpose of the Hague-Visby rules. What are the rules and which Act contains them?

- What are the shipping documents? Could you summarise their differing functions?

- What is a letter of credit and how does it work in practice?

- What are the different types of letter of credit?

International Sale of Goods

- What is the purpose of the Uniform Laws on International Sales Act 1967?

- What rules apply governing formation of the contract and its contents?

Arbitration

- What is meant by arbitration and how does it differ from mediation?
- What are the advantages and disadvantages of arbitration over litigation?
- Is it possible to appeal against an arbitration award?
- What is meant by a Scott Avery clause?
- How did the Arbitration Act 1996 change the procedural rules relating to arbitration?
- What additional benefits and disadvantages apply when arbitration is used in international disputes?

Intellectual Property Rights

(specifically confidentiality, passing off and contractual provisions)

- What are the 3 requirements for a successful confidentiality claim?
- What is meant by 'confidential information'?
- What tests are used to decide where there is a duty not to confide?
- What happened in Saltman Engineering v Campbell and what was the outcome?
- What are the two possible bases of claim on which confidentiality actions can be brought?
- What happened in Seager V Copydex Ltd (or Coco v Clark Engineers Ltd) and what was the outcome?
- In what circumstances can an employer restrict an employee's use of information during and after he is employed by him?
- What happened in Faccenda Chicken Co Ltd v Fowler and what was the outcome?
- What is meant by the economic tort of 'passing off'? (definitions)
- What is meant by 'get up'?
- What happened in Hoffman La Roche v DDSA and what was the outcome?
- What happened in Maxim v Dye and what was the outcome?

- What is meant by 'common field of activity'?

- What happened in Wombles Ltd v Wombles Skips and what was the outcome?

- What happened in Lego v Lemelstrich and what was the outcome?

- What type of damage is recoverable under passing off actions?

- What happened in Harrods Ltd v R. Harrod Ltd and what was the outcome?

- What happened in Bollinger v Costa Brava Wine Co (and Erven Warninck v Townend) and what were the outcomes?

- What are the key issues relating to IPR that must be dealt with in a contract?

- What provisions should be included in a contract to encourage respect for confidentiality of information and other IPR?

Index